"In *From Talent Management to Talent Liberat*
challenge organisational leaders to reflect on
strategies and step back from the process to the
strike an excellent balance between insights fror.
examples in identifying the key questions whic
The result is a thoughtful analysis which will   .... practitioner
to ensure that talent management can liberate the potential in their talent and
deliver on the talent agenda in the new workplace. It is essential reading for any
talent practitioner."

– **David G. Collings**, Professor of HRM,
Dublin City University Business School, Ireland.

"What is in a word? The authors highlight the assumptions we make and
prescriptions we follow when managing talent. They use the metaphor of talent
liberation to show us how to link improvements in our practice to a challenging
business context. This is the book for those who accept the need for critical
thinking but are also looking for positive and practical ways forward."

– **Paul Sparrow**, Emeritus Professor of International
HRM, Lancaster University Management School, UK.

"Peoples' talents and learning flourish when liberated and, like the genie, they
refuse to be put back in the bottle."

– **Dr Peter Honey**, Occupational Psychologist &
Management Trainer, UK.

This guide to 'talent liberation' is a fluent and nicely thought-provoking read, with
a practical tone and a clear structure. It usefully pulls together a set of ideas that
reflective practitioners have been moving towards, challenging the often lazy 'war
for talent' rhetoric. The over-emphasis on formal HR procedures is called out and
counter-balanced by advice for leaders on how to grow their teams. Useful models
make the crucial links between talent management and workforce planning on the
one hand and how individuals develop their own careers on the other."

– **Wendy Hirsh**, Principal Associate, Institute for
Employment Studies, UK.

"This book offers a critical analysis of talent management. Adopting the
metaphor of talent liberation, the authors offer a path forward for talent
management better fitted to projected trends concerning the future of work. I
found the use of cases and the explicit identification of practical implications
for HR departments, leaders, and individual employees especially useful. In
addition, the book sets out to help bridge the scientist-practitioner gap in talent
management, another issue that is hindering the field from progressing forward.
I applaud any and all effort to approach this topic area from a critical and
bridging perspective, as this book does so well."

– **Nicky Dries**, Research Professor of Organizational Behavior,
KU Leuven & BI Norwegian Business School, Norway.

"The authors have done a remarkable job summarizing and extending ideas around talent liberation. Beyond simple solutions, they offer unique and relevant ways to liberate the skills and energy of people in organizations. They help leaders move beyond idealistic calls for talent to specific actions to get the most out of talent."

— **Dave Ulrich**, Rensis Likert Professor, Ross School of Business, University of Michigan Partner, USA.

"Whilst carefully grounded in the literature, this is very much a practical book, offering useable tools and examples, based in part on the authors' research and consulting work with clients. There is no simple "best practice" model on offer; instead the authors guide us through a set of questions designed to help develop a "talent liberation" approach appropriate to the context, strategy and culture of the organization. Specific guidance is also provided to help HR, leaders, and individuals themselves liberate talent. Engaging and useful, this book is a must have for those involved in the practice of talent management."

— **Ed Snape**, Dean & Chair Professor in Management, School of Business, Hong Kong Baptist University, Hong Kong.

"Steeped in significant research, thought leadership and current practical examples, *From Talent Management to Talent Liberation* provides new direction for understanding how we unleash talent for our age. These highly qualified authors propose a flexible 5-part framework, sets of questions, and tools that help you, your leaders, and your organization craft your best opportunities for uncovering and encouraging talent to thrive in today's complex work environment. This is a breakthrough approach to the most important aspects of maximizing talent."

— **Wendy Axelrod**, PhD, Executive Coach and Mentor, USA.

From Talent Management to Talent Liberation

As the pace of change increases and new business structures evolve, finding and harnessing people's talent is becoming ever more important. *From Talent Management to Talent Liberation* presents a thoughtful and practical approach to talent. It provides compelling evidence for the limitations of talent management practice and offers talent liberation as an alternative approach.

Talent Liberation is positioned through five premises that draw on the agile movement to provide a fundamental reappraisal of the talent agenda. These premises are then applied through a range of strategic and tactical tools such as the Talent Compass. By combining academic research, thought leadership and practical experience, this book will stimulate fresh thinking.

Readers will be inspired to take action, using the simple tools to liberate more of the talent in their organisation and their teams. Leaders, HR professionals and individuals will benefit from the relevant insights shared here.

Maggi Evans is an influential consultant with extensive international experience of strategy, senior leadership, change and talent. Focused on building competitive advantage, she is committed to translating academic insights into pragmatic business solutions.

John Arnold is Professor of Organisational Behaviour at the School of Business and Economics, Loughborough University, UK. John's influential research, teaching and consultancy involve all areas of careers and their management, from both individual and organizational perspectives.

Andrew Rothwell is Director of MSc Human Resource Management programmes at Loughborough University, UK. Andrew has extensive experience of leadership, professional development and consultancy across a range of industries. He has research interests in CPD and employability.

From Talent Management to Talent Liberation

A Practical Guide for Professionals, Managers and Leaders

Maggi Evans
with John Arnold and
Andrew Rothwell

Routledge
Taylor & Francis Group

LONDON AND NEW YORK

First published 2020
by Routledge
2 Park Square, Milton Park, Abingdon, Oxon OX14 4RN

and by Routledge
52 Vanderbilt Avenue, New York, NY 10017

Routledge is an imprint of the Taylor & Francis Group, an informa business

British Library Cataloguing-in-Publication Data
A catalogue record for this book is available from the British Library

Library of Congress Cataloging-in-Publication Data
A catalog record for this book has been requested

ISBN: 978-0-367-23306-8 (hbk)
ISBN: 978-0-367-23298-6 (pbk)
ISBN: 978-0-429-27920-1 (ebk)

Typeset in Bembo
by Apex CoVantage, LLC
Printed and bound by CPI Group (UK) Ltd, Croydon, CR0 4YY

Paperback cover image design: Joke De Winter

To my amazing family – Dave, Sam, Lily and Fred. Thank you for your endless love, support and laughter.

Maggi

Contents

Figures and tables

Figures

Tables

Preface

Interest in talent management has grown hugely, sparking new job titles, conferences, numerous books, articles and thought leadership pieces. The rhetoric has been that talent is scarce and organisations need to make sure that they secure the best possible talent as the only way to survive and grow in the turbulent world they are in. The phrase 'war for talent' is spoken in many global board rooms.

Twenty years have now passed since the start of this war, and there is no sign of peace breaking out. The approach to talent management that many organisations have adopted isn't bringing the promised results. CEOs have consistently expressed their concerns, and in candid moments HR professionals also say that talent management is running away with them, developing a life of its own. As one Chief People Officer told us recently, 'we've got so wrapped up in the processes of talent management we've forgotten what its purpose is'. We tend to concur with this. We see a lot of angst and concern about recruiting talented people, how to identify them, how to best develop them and how to make sure that they stay . . . but despite all the hours spent on it, is it really benefitting anyone other than the consultants?

In this book we recognise some of the good things about talent management but also take a critical view of the way it is practised in many organisations. In particular, we show how current approaches are ill-equipped to add value in the evolving world of work. We argue that not only are many talent management practices no longer fit for purpose, but they can create negative unintended consequences. However, the fundamental contribution of talent management (broadly to safeguard business continuity through ensuring ongoing access to well motivated and appropriately skilled/experienced workforce) remains a critical activity. We provide an alternative perspective on how this can be achieved. Our perspective broadens the scope of talent management:

- from a focus on process to a focus on purpose
- from a single focus on the organisation's needs to one that balances these with individual aspiration
- from a preoccupation with individual performance to an awareness of the importance of team performance
- from an organisation-driven approach to one that involves, empowers and engages the individual.

We are not saying this is easy. However, through tools, examples, illustrations and questions we aim to guide and encourage you to take some steps towards a new approach.

The book has a simple structure that should enable you to read the whole story or dip in and out of as you need. Part I (the first three chapters) sets the context, and then we move into practical application. Chapter 1 provides a summary of the current state of talent management – where it has come from, the successes and the challenges of current practice. We also use this chapter to describe what we mean when we say 'talent' and 'talent management'. Chapter 2 explores some of the ways in which the world of work seems to be evolving and the implications of this for talent management. Having shown the limitations of current approaches, Chapter 3 introduces the metaphor of talent liberation, a 'nudge' to open up new ways of thinking about talent that reflects organisations of the future. Five premises of talent liberation are introduced, showing how they contribute to our thinking and overcome some of the challenges of talent management described in Chapter 1.

Part II (chapters 4 to 7) focuses on the practice of talent liberation. This starts with the introduction of a tool, the Talent Compass. This will help you to map the whole of your talent system, building a picture of how the different parts interact, what your key risks are and how to start planning how to address these. The following chapters provide more detail on taking this approach with lots of examples and mini case studies. Chapter 5 focuses on the role that HR can take in liberating talent, followed by Chapter 6 looking at the role of the leader as talent liberator and Chapter 7 exploring how you personally can take action to liberate more of your own talent.

Part III provides a toolkit with some additional resources to help you to apply the talent liberation approach within your own organisation.

We believe that this book is timely. Talent management is now a well-established field, but there is a lack of sharing between the academic and practitioner literatures. Academics have been debating some of the issues raised in this book for a number of years. Meanwhile the practitioner field has been sharing ideas and views on best practice and often, in our view, making grand and unsubstantiated claims about the benefits of talent management. But now CEOs and HR professionals seem to be questioning current approaches, feeling that they aren't working.[1]

As we have been writing this book, we have been struck by the cyclical nature of thinking in leadership and management. We therefore make no apology that many of the ideas and approaches we suggest have already 'been round the block'. In our quest for what's new, we often forget some of the sage advice of the past – until it re-emerges with a bright and shiny new label. Wherever possible we have credited the earlier thinking that we draw on.

In collaborating on this book, we have had four main aims:

- Providing a bridge between academic and practitioner thinking
- Showing that the current approach to talent management is too narrow to bring the competitive advantage it aims to deliver, particularly given the evolving changes in the world of work

- Introducing alternative ways of thinking about talent management that can open up new ways of attracting, selecting, developing, deploying and retaining talented people
- Providing practical ways to adopt a new talent agenda whether you are an HR professional, a leader, or someone who wants to liberate more of their own talent

Our goal has been to provide a new blueprint for talent that is simple, practical, credible and inspirational.

We recognise that the word 'talent' is used in a variety of ways. Where possible we have respected that talent is a personal attribute and have described 'talented people'. At times however, when referring to people collectively, it was easier and clearer to use 'talent' as an abstract noun and refer to 'the talent'. We do not wish this to imply a lack of respect for those being described in this way.

Throughout the book we refer to research that 'we' have conducted and conversations that 'we' have had. In most instances this was conducted by one of us rather than all three of us together.[2]

Notes

1 For example, see the PwC CEO survey, www.pwc.com/gx/en/ceo-agenda/ceosur vey/2017/gx/deep-dives/the-talent-challenge.html, Manpower Group talent review, http://manpowergroup.com/talent-shortage-2016 and Deloitte review of human capital trends, https://www2.deloitte.com/global/en/pages/human-capital/articles/introduction-human-capital-trends.html (all accessed 30.04.2019).
2 For example, much of the practical work and case studies are drawn from Maggi's consulting experience.

Acknowledgements

Many people have contributed to this book. We are grateful to those who have offered us their insights into talent and talent liberation, to those who have been willing to provide case studies which are shared in this book, to those who have provided feedback on the content and to those who have been involved in testing out the many tools presented in the following chapters. Thank you.

- Alan Lawless
- Alistair Cox
- Andrew Russell
- Anne-Marie Hearne
- Caroline Littleton
- Caroline Sledge
- Charlotte Black
- Chloe Upston
- Chloe Clayton
- Christie Taylor
- Christina Chronister
- Clare Vintner
- Clare Kemsley
- Craig McCoy
- Eleanor Reedy
- Emma Crowe
- Harish Natali
- Helen Green
- Hilary Rapinet
- Hugo Pound
- Iain Coyne
- Jackie Switzer
- Jamie Garner
- Jayne Mee
- Jeff Hewitt
- Kay Maybin
- Kenton Bradbury
- Kirstie White
- Lisa Ashdown
- Lottie Evans
- Lucy Standing
- Marc Bena
- Marie Power
- Mark Shrimpton
- Mervyn Potter
- Molly Selby
- Nick Bradley
- Nikki Kaur
- Peter Honey
- Polly Davison
- Ralph Berg
- Richard Alexander
- Richard Eardley
- Richard Springer
- Sally Bibb
- Sandra Henke
- Sanjay Bhogaita
- Sarah-Jane Last
- Sarah Kilvington
- Sarah Turton

- Jenni Waller
- John Richards
- Jonathan Males
- Jonathon Brown
- Jonathan Musselwhite
- Julie Chell
- Julie Kirk

- Shetel Khimashia
- Simon Downing
- Simon Scoggins
- Sue White
- Vicky Holdsworth
- Vince Chaney
- Wendy Merry

We would also like to thank all of the people who have shared their career and talent stories with us as part of our ongoing research.

Part I

The context for talent liberation

1 Talent management – not fit for purpose

Introduction

There have been numerous warnings about the impact of a forthcoming talent crisis. For example, the recently published Korn Ferry paper ('*The Global Talent Crunch*') described a 2030 scenario with a global talent shortage of 85.2 million people, impacting global revenue by a staggering $8.45 trillion. The availability of key skills remains a top-five concern for CEOs[1] – only just behind over-regulation, terrorism, geopolitical uncertainty and cyberthreats. Millennials, as relatively new entrants to the workforce, often find themselves overqualified, underemployed, unsatisfied and inclined to move on or quit.[2] It is these issues that talent management is positioned as helping us with. Since the mid-1990s the idea has been that by looking at resourcing needs across the employee life cycle we can potentially mitigate the risks of the talent crisis.

What do we mean by talent?

It's very easy to use the word talent, but what do we actually mean by it?

Key questions to consider

- Does everyone have talent or just a select few?
- Is it innate, or can it be developed?
- Is it about being better than others or the best you can be?
- How does talent relate to performance and potential?
- Is talent a general quality or specific to a job or organisation?
- Is it possible to measure someone's talent?
- Does individual motivation influence how talented we are perceived to be?

So what is talent? Is it innate, or can it be developed? Can talent be hired? Is it something that a 'talented' individual can replicate in different settings? We have reviewed the academic and leadership literature and found numerous interpretations of talent and many apparent contradictions.[3] Interestingly, some writers draw on the same examples to make opposite points. For example, Mozart is cited as an example of both the innate and developed elements of talent.[4] Cultural differences in the way the word is used have also been observed. For example, in the West there is a tendency to view talent as largely innate, whereas in Japan, there is a dominant view that talent is developed as a result of intense and disciplined training.[5] To make sense of these different views of talent, we have found it helpful to consider them initially in terms of two questions: first, how rare is talent? (from everyone having talent to just the select few); second, to what extent (are you born with talent, or is it developed?) We have presented this as a 2 × 2 matrix (Figure 1.1), which presents four potential descriptions of talent.[6] We refer to this as the Talent Quadrants, and the labels attached to each quadrant are used throughout the book.

Those who consider talent as rare and exclusive often refer to the 'A' players, or in Tomas Chamorro-Premuzic's language, 'the vital few'.[7] This is typically

Figure 1.1 Talent quadrants

positioned as the top 10–20% of people in particular roles (either already per-forming in this way or with the potential to perform in this way). It is argued that it is important to be clear who these people are so they receive greater investment. This investment may come in the form of attraction, development and retention strategies, justified on the basis that these people are strategically important and make a particularly strong contribution to the success of the busi-ness. Thus, for advocates of this view, talent management is equated to a decision science of how and where to invest.[8] Within this exclusive view of talent, those who see it as largely stable are likely to focus on assessing personality, cognitive strengths and motivations and to use past performance in order to establish who is 'gifted' in a particular field. Those who see talent as developable will be keen to establish the high potential someone has so that this can be developed and deployed.

On the other hand, the inclusive approach represents a commitment to get the best possible contribution from everyone in the organisation. As such, this positions talent management with a similar ethos to HR management, finding ways to improve the attraction, selection, recruitment, deployment, development and engagement of all employees in order to support the strategic aims of the organisation. Those who see inclusive talent as largely stable are likely to engage with activities to uncover personal strengths and to look for the attitudes and behaviours that come naturally. Once these strengths are understood, individuals can be deployed in roles that will be intrinsically motivating for them.[9] Those who adopt an inclusive and developable view of talent look to encourage every-one in the organisation to become exceptional performers. This is achieved through ongoing development and supporting a 'growth mindset'[10] whereby people actively invest in and promote their own learning.

The definition or philosophy chosen – inclusive or exclusive, developable or stable – will shape the talent management processes which are adopted and how they are implemented. This will influence the way they are received by employ-ees, which in turn has been found to influence the impact such processes have.[11] Proponents of each of the four philosophies outlined earlier claim benefits and competitive advantage. However, each definition can also be associated with shortcomings and implementation challenges.

What of our other questions regarding talent? Analysing the talent quadrants enables the following insights:

Is talent about being better than others or about being your Personal Best?
If talent is viewed as exclusive (High Potential or Gifted), it follows that the evidence for talent is being in some way 'better' than others (interpersonal). If, however, an inclusive view is taken, then talent is about being the best you can be (intrapersonal).

How does talent relate to performance and potential?
Those who equate talent with being Gifted are likely to view performance as the key indicator of talent. Those who take a High Potential view will

attempt to find ways to spot potential, seeing this as the key indicator of talent. They will then aim to invest in development activities in order to translate the latent potential into superior performance. Some people may have already made this transition and be considered as 'ready now' talent. For those with a Strengths view, potential is released into superior performance when someone has an opportunity to use their natural strengths in their work. For the Personal Best proponents, development potential is especially important and is the gap between where someone is currently performing and how things would be if they were at their own peak performance.

Is talent a general quality or specific to a job or organisation?
Talent is normally specific to different domains of human functioning, so talent in one setting may not indicate talent in another area. These domains can be defined by different levels of specificity. You may have two talented musicians. However, it may be difficult to compare their talent as they are each talented in their own domain (say one as a pianist and the other as a singer). In the work context, two talented leaders can have very different skills. Someone good at rescuing a failing operation in America may not be well suited to starting a new office in the APAC region. The skills required for each task are valuable but likely to be different.

Is it possible to measure talent?
There are lots of ways of measuring talent, but the choice of measures will depend on what you mean by talent. One is more likely to find reliable measures if talent is seen as a fairly stable quality (taking either a Strengths or a Gifted perspective). This leads to the use of psychometric measures of cognitive ability, personality, motivations and core strengths. However, those who see talent as developable (Personal Best or High Potential) are also keen to find measures of people's potential. In spite of this complexity, it has been suggested[12] that potential can be assessed by reference to three dimensions: *foundations* (the more stable aspects such as cognitive abilities and personality); *growth* (the ways in which someone can adapt, learn and grow); and *career* (skills and motivations which indicate suitability to certain career areas).

Does motivation influence talent?
In the talent context, people's motivation has been described as 'activities they like, find important and in which they want to invest energy in'.[13] This seems likely to be an important part of talent whichever description is adopted. For example, someone could be Gifted in a particular area, but without motivation to apply their gift, it is unlikely that excellent performance will be achieved. For the Strengths approach, motivation is a key element, with people being more intrinsically motivated when they are free to use their strengths in their work. For Personal Best and High Potential views of talent, motivation is a critical element of someone's desire to grow and develop to translate their potential into talent.

These different interpretations of talent are not of themselves right or wrong. Nor are they mutually exclusive; indeed it is possible to combine the different definitions, depending on organisational needs. However, many organisations do not define what they mean by talent, using it in a vague way.[14] It is assumed that people know what is meant and that they all mean the same thing, but this tends not to be explored or made explicit. This creates difficulties in selecting the most appropriate purpose, approach and tools of talent management.

Sport has invested considerable time and research in working out the best ways to identify and develop talent. 'The Talent Lab'[15] provides a fascinating account of the approach taken by the British Olympic team to prepare for the 2012 (and subsequent) Olympics. They were very clear on the physical attributes that needed to already be there (the innate traits), such as fast muscle twitch for sprinters and aerial awareness for divers. They were also clear on the skills that could be learned – broadening their sources of potential talent. They were also focused on the motivational aspects, including the capacity to learn, and exploring what 'headroom' the person had to grow.

This programme has been credited with huge success, including taking people such as Lizzy Yarnold (skeleton gold at Sochi, 2014) and Helen Glover (rowing gold in the coxless pairs, London, 2012) to gold medals within a few years of starting new sports.

What is talent management, and what has it contributed?

The term 'talent management' emerged in the 1990s. Initially talent management activities were targeted to ensure a secure and sustainable succession plan of people to the most important positions in an organisation (typically the most senior roles but also including some highly technical and hard-to-recruit-for roles). Gradually the scope increased to include longer-term people planning and existing programmes (such as graduate schemes and middle management development). Research has indicated four core approaches to talent management, based on the perceived source of competitive advantage:[16]

- People – focusing on star performers (a focus on people considered to be High Potential and the identification, attraction, development and retention of these people)
- Practices – focusing on the benefit of adherence to excellent practice and process (which can relate to any of the talent definitions and typically include assessment, succession planning, career pathways and leadership development and an increasing interest in employer branding, structured career moves and programmes to encourage diversity)
- Key positions – focusing on the key positions (not just leadership) that are critical to organisational success (which can relate to any of the talent definitions and manages business risk by securing availability of suitably qualified people to perform in key roles)

- Strategic talent pools – focusing on groupings or clusters of talent and preparing them to meet future organisational demands (which can include any of the talent definitions but generally focuses on people considered to have High Potential for a variety of roles, for example, groups of graduates or people with particular technology skills)

Many organisations use a combination of these approaches. For example, they may combine a 'High Potential' and 'Personal Best' description of talent. They may focus on a people approach but be very structured in the practices that they apply. Some of these combinations can be seen in the following examples.

'For us, everyone has talent, and we want to develop them to be the best they can be. We also see a particular group of people as high potential, and we provide some specific development opportunities to them so that they can move into the most important roles'.

HR Director, Financial Services

'Talent management is about managing a select group of people who have the potential to make a massive difference to the business'.

HR Director, Construction

'Our talent management programme is about moving resources across and through the organisation, having appropriate career frameworks to fast-track to senior roles so we have capability in the right places. It's about getting the right people in the right job at the right time, planning for gaps with succession planning, having actions to fill any gaps and knowing where we may have gaps in the future'.

HR Director, Global Services

As with the definition of talent, we do not see there as being a right and a wrong way. Rather we suggest that the approach adopted should be consistent with the needs of the organisation. Thus, within this book, we offer a variety of perspectives and approaches. We aim to be transparent about which approaches we are applying at any time. However, we recognise that we do have a preference for the idea that talent is developable; thus we tend to favour approaches that fit with the Personal Best or High Potential descriptions of talent. Similarly, whilst we see the importance of some practices that support having the 'best employees in the most strategic roles',[17] we tend to be somewhat critical of their contribution (as we shall discuss later in this chapter).

While we are critical of existing talent approaches, we also recognise the contribution that talent management has brought to the field of HR. At an organisational level, this has included bringing a strategic focus to the recruitment, management, development and retention of people, focusing attention on skills for the future, introducing greater rigour around succession planning and encouraging greater diversity. At national and international level, talent management has contributed insights regarding talent shortages in specific professions (health, engineering and IT) and ways of understanding the changing global labour market.

There are also many very strong case studies which demonstrate the positive outcomes that can arise from a well thought-out, contextualised approach to talent management, including inspirational examples from HSBC, Google and Coca Cola.[18] Often there is a strong evidence base to demonstrate the value or return on investment that talent management has brought, and a compelling case is made. For us, these case studies demonstrate that in certain circumstances, it is possible for talent management to make a significant contribution.

At the same time, there are three reasons why we urge caution. First, there is a lack of strong evidence base for talent management consistently providing a return on investment.[19] Indeed, our own research indicates that the main way in which organisations measure the impact of talent management is the existence of a succession plan. Second, the successes are often attributed to a talent management process, but there could have been a number of other features of the organisation, culture or people that contributed to the success. This leads people to focus on implementing process with little regard for other factors, which could be just as influential. Third, we tend to be somewhat sceptical of many of the presented case studies. This was well articulated by a senior talent director from a large global organisation:

'Despite the flaws, if I were to write this up as a case study, it could look very impressive – we have succession planning at three levels; a talent identification programme; the capabilities are well articulated; we have partners for assessments – but if you were to ask people how they experience the process and the contribution that it really makes to the business, you would get a very different view'.

Talent Director, Global Financial Services

The challenges

As you'd expect (from the title of the book, if nothing else), as well as recognising some of the contributions of talent management, we also see a number of challenges. Together these lead to a lack of understanding of organisation's future talent needs and a disconnect from business strategy. We believe that many of these problems with talent management are not about the theoretical principles but are flaws in the way it is interpreted and operationalised within organisations. So rather than go into a long list of all we think is wrong, we share with you five of our main concerns. We do not claim these as our own; rather we present them to you as a curated list, drawn from writers such as Jeffery Pfeffer, Malcolm Gladwell, Rob Briner, Bob Sutton, David Collings and others, with a bit of flavour added by some of our research, observations and experiences.

Mindset of scarcity

> 'We talk about potential, and the same five names keep coming up. It seems as if we don't have a talent pool; we have a talent puddle'!
>
> HR Director, Global Technology Business

We are very familiar with the rhetoric of shortages, whether of skilled workers, commodities or natural resources. The language of a 'war for talent' feeds straight into this, with scary headlines about the potential impact on our economy. Fears of shortages can have both positive and negative consequences. Thinking positively, shortages can drive innovation. (Think of how concern of oil shortages has been a catalyst for energy efficiency and advances in renewable energy.) However, a mindset of scarcity can also have negative effects.

Firstly, there are changes in the market with prices going up. This has certainly been the case with belief in a limited supply of qualified executives seemingly leading to huge increase in executive pay. For example, a long-running study by the AFL-CIO illustrates the widening pay gap between leaders and other production/non-supervisory employees, with the differential nine times higher in 2018 than in 1983.[20] Are these leaders really worth it? Does the mindset of limited talent justify very high and increasing executive pay? Secondly, because of familiarity with the scarcity story, the headlines are rarely scrutinised to challenge the data. We suggest that the headline statistics on talent shortages are just one version of the future, with many variables such as technological change, political change and demographics not accounted for. Furthermore, these assumptions tend to be global- or industry-based and probably don't represent the needs or context of your particular organisation. Our third concern is the impact of a scarcity mindset on thinking about new sources of talent supply. In their fascinating book on scarcity,[21] Harvard economics professor Sendhil Mullainathan and Princeton psychology professor Eldar Shafir illustrate how, when things are scarce, we fixate on what we've not got. They describe it as a loss of bandwidth, whereby our ability to judge situations reduces and we fail to see the bigger picture. This seems to be at play in organisations. As we shall describe in Chapter 3, many organisations have considerable underutilised talent, ready and waiting. However, having been told that talent is scarce, many managers feel that they need to keep hold of talented people in their team, restricting movement of people, reducing development opportunities and ultimately contributing to a lack of talent.

Cult of individual heroes

> 'Performance can cloud judgement on potential. There's a real seduction of results. Time and time again, you see a type of hero worship and then surprise when the hero fails in something else'.
>
> HR Director, Global FMCG

Many of the talent management processes organisations adopt are based on an assumption that the right leader in the right place will create the best possible results. Moreover, in order to win, you need to make sure that the best people are working for you, not your competitors.[22] In some instances this is surely the case. For example, leaders who fit the description of 'multipliers' (based on research by Liz Wiseman and Greg McKeown)[23] create an environment where everyone performs better, where talent is attracted, engaged and developed for the future. However, looking at unsuccessful organisations, it is possible to see that acquiring a highly talented CEO is no guarantee of success. There have been many public examples of seemingly talented CEOs leading their organisations to failure. The influential psychologist Adrian Furnham cites the Institute for Policy Studies as identifying 38% of the 241 highest-paid CEOs as poor performers who were 'bailed out, booted or busted'.[24]

We suggest that the cult of individual heroes can be risky and problematic. There seems to be a preference for people who are seen to 'fit in' and who have made their achievements visible to those who will be charged with making decisions about their future. There are clear risks in these preferences. Firstly, they reduce diversity of background, skills, character and thinking. This focuses organisations on all looking for the same people in the same places – homogeneous talent management instead of inclusive talent management.[25] If you are operating in a stable environment, this may not matter. However, organisations that look to their talent to provide fresh thinking may risk selecting it out and actively avoiding disruptive talent.[26] Secondly, heroes are rewarded for being self-promoting, but such behaviours may be the opposite of what you really want and need at the top. Research helpfully differentiates between two aspects of leadership, labelling them as leadership emergence (standing out, influencing others, building connections) and leadership effectiveness (leading the business, managing resources, leading people).[27] Successful leaders need both, but heroes may be rewarded for their leadership emergence, whilst others are overlooked. Thirdly, the attribution of success to the leader rather than the team or the context also creates a 'halo' effect around leaders.[28] If they have been the leader when spectacular success was achieved, we assume that they are highly capable and will be able to repeat the success in another situation. This doesn't necessarily follow, the 'hero' may not live up to expectations and unsurprisingly may fail to deliver the expected results (as indicated by the 'bailed out, booted or busted' figures quoted earlier).

Lack of strategic clarity

> 'Our organisation is constantly changing and evolving. It's hard to know what's going to happen next, so how can we truly define our future people and talent needs?'
>
> HR Director, Global Technology

As described earlier, the logic of talent management depends on the 'best' person in the 'most strategic roles' and preparing a 'pipeline' of talent for the future. However, organisations tend to invest little time in exploring what the 'most strategic roles' are, who the 'best' person might be and what the future needs are in terms of necessary skills, experiences, behaviours and motivations. These needs can vary considerably by organisation. For example, an organisation that prioritises the strategic value of customer intimacy, will look for different people than an organisation that prioritises product leadership or organisational efficiency.[29] Without this insight, it is difficult for HR to make future focused decisions on the talent needs. However, many HR functions seem locked in administrative roles, rather than engaging in building strategic insight into future talent needs.[30] This lack of clarity undermines the quality of discussions about potential, leaving a key question hanging in the air 'potential for what'?

Whilst books and articles state that linking talent management to strategy is an important step[31] (sometimes with a timeframe as long as 15 years) the specifics of how organisations can do this tend to be somewhat vague. The organisations that do attempt to define these talent requirements find it difficult to be clear. This is not surprising given that strategic experts such as Bain & Company[32] are increasingly suggesting that strategy should be viewed more as fast adaptation, rather than perfect prediction. Others, such as Professor Ralph Stacey question the dominant management paradigm that strategy is developed by the senior leaders and then implemented within the organisation. Rather, he points to a more emergent view of the organisation whereby all elements of the organisational system interact in numerous, small ways (leaders, team members, products, markets, customers etc.). The combined effect of these local interactions is change to the whole system – change which is impossible to predict or to 'manage'. He suggests that the role of strategy is to influence the evolution of the whole system through communication and interactions. These alternative views present a challenge for talent management which has largely employed practices based on predictable needs and static environments.[33] These are ill-suited to the evolving world of work that we explore in Chapter 2.

Dominance of formal process

> 'I have worked somewhere where there was a very structured process, the same across the world. We had a very prescriptive way of doing talent management. But there was a huge disconnect between the rhetoric and the reality'.
>
> HR Director Financial Services

Talent management, like other parts of management, has become pre-occupied with control which drives adoption of many processes. Many of these are implemented with great intentions. For example, the use of competency frameworks is often driven by a desire for consistency, fairness and transparency. Succession planning is often put in place to manage organisational risk, and processes of appraisal and review are there to support clarity of priorities and monitoring of performance. But often these processes have unintended consequences. The rules and processes that are put in place keep ownership with the HR function. They push HR into a policing role to make sure things are done, trapping them into the administrative role mentioned previously. Meanwhile, managers, leaders and individuals 'play the game'. They are often (after some nagging) compliant, but the positive intentions and the benefits get lost along the way. Indeed, as mentioned in the introduction, one HR Director recognised the problem and summarised it by saying 'we've got so focused on the process that we've forgotten about the purpose'.

These problems seem endemic. When we ask HR professionals about talent management, they typically reply by listing the processes they apply. Succession plans dominate, often using input from the nine-box grid which illustrates where people sit on a performance/potential matrix.[34] Outputs from the process are often development opportunities (particularly coaching and mentoring) and sometimes additional projects or secondments to provide some missing experiences. However, when the actual talent management activities are reviewed, it's difficult to see how they combine to provide an integrated approach and how this can possibly deliver the aims of talent management – to attract, select, develop, deploy and retain these highly desirable employees. It seems that much of the energy is focused on reporting and monitoring rather than improving and gaining competitive advantage.

Moreover, this dominance of formal talent management processes risks a lack of attention to other features of the organisation that can enable strong talent management. The organisational context is a crucial influence on how the formal processes will create impact. This importance of context in talent management has been recognised by many academics[35] and extends to elements of culture, structure, decision making and other processes. One academic paper captures this as 'issues of focus and fit',[36] highlighting the need for the talent management approach to 'fit' the organisational culture. For example, not to rely on open feedback and conversations if that is not part of the prevailing culture; not to keep confidential lists if the culture of the organisation is high on transparency.

Missing half the story

> 'Our focus is always about what the organisation wants and needs. We're not very good at finding out what the talented individual wants – we assume it's all about the promotion'.
>
> HR Director, Global Financial Services

Referring back to our earlier question 'does motivation influence talent' we identified the importance of the motivational aspects of what the person likes, finds important and wants to do. However, within most organisations, individual hopes and motivations are rarely a main consideration of talent management,[37] hence missing an opportunity to align these with the goals of the organisation. Some recognise this gap and do engage in some attempts to find out what an individual wants (often through development centres or line manager led conversations). However, the HR people we speak with feel that such data are unreliable. This seems to be largely as a result of lack of trust. Individuals are perceived as playing the game and giving the answer they think they should rather than having an honest conversation. The consequences of this misalignment are potentially huge and costly. For example, some organisations include someone on the succession plan for an overseas role, only to find that they are not interested in relocating or someone being promoted to a new role which they hate and as a result they leave the organisation. These issues are a central theme in the recently published 'Talent Playbook', which suggests that the future of talent management requires organisations to genuinely put their people first and use this to drive direction and strategy.[38]

However, we recognise that there are challenges to be overcome in order to create an environment where individuals will openly share their aspirations. The way many talent processes are enacted can be seen to undermine an agenda of alignment. For example, there tends to be a lack of transparency or trust from the organisation to the individual, with few organisations sharing their assessment of potential or the succession plans with the individual concerned.[39] These barriers form part of the organisational context discussed earlier.

Reflections

In this chapter we have set out our definitions of talent and talent management. We have shown some of the benefits of that talent management can bring, before sharing our concerns. We summarise our concerns by suggesting that in most organisations, talent management is not fit for purpose. The way it is applied is too narrow to bring the competitive advantage it aims to deliver.

You may find the following questions helpful as you reflect on your current approach to talent management.

- How do you define talent in your organisation (High Potential, Personal Best, Strengths, Gifted)?
- What are the aims of talent management in your organisation?
- How do you apply the people, practices, key positions and talent pool approaches?
- How do you measure the impact of your approach?
- In what ways do you have a scarcity mindset in your organisation, and what is the impact of this?
- In what ways do you engage in the cult of the hero, and what is the impact of this?
- How do you understand your future needs, and how flexible is this?
- How do your formal processes match the context?
- How do you ensure you involve talented people within your talent approach?
- To what extent is your current talent management approach fit for purpose?

Notes

1 See www.pwc.com/gx/en/ceo-survey/2018/pwc-ceo-survey-report-2018.pdf (accessed 28.06.2019).
2 See the CIPD Employee Outlook, 2017 for further information, www.cipd.co.uk/Images/employee-outlook_2017-spring_tcm18-21163.pdf (accessed 24.04.2019).
3 For example, Thunnissen et al. (2013) reviewed sixty-two academic articles and found that half of them had no clear description of talent or definition of talent management. Thunnissen, M., Boselie, P. and Fruytier, B., 2013. A review of talent management: 'Infancy or adolescence?' *The International Journal of Human Resource Management* 24(9), 1744–1761.
4 Mozart is often cited as an example of someone showing a genuine gift or talent for a particular skill. For example, Tomas Chamorro-Premuzic, in his book, 2017. *The Talent Delusion*. London: Piatkus, defines talent as 'effortless performance' and goes on to refer to 'raw talent', putting Mozart in this category. He cites the evidence of Mozart being just five when he published his first composition, showing a remarkable level of performance without the opportunity to benefit from significant practise over time (see page 47). However, Geoff Colvin, in his book *Talent is Overrated* (London: Nicholas Brealey, 2016) introduces an alternative perspective, suggesting that Mozart's father (himself a famous composer) was very ambitious for his son and gave him intensive training. The early compositions were also 'corrected' by the father before being seen by others and that many of his early compositions are arrangements of previously published work rather than original. Mozart was twenty-one when his first masterpiece was published.

5 Tansley, C., 2011. What do we mean by the term "talent" in talent management? *Industrial and Commercial Training* 43(5), 266–274.

6 These were identified as underlying talent philosophies in: Meyers, M. C. and Van Woerkom, M., 2014. The influence of underlying philosophies on talent management: Theory, implications for practice, and research agenda. *Journal of World Business* 49(2), 192–203. The format for this diagram was adapted from a presentation by Nicky Dries at University of Loughborough, UK, in April.

7 Tomas Chamorro-Premuzic (see endnote 4) relates this to Pareto's law of economics that 20 percent of the workforce produces 80 percent of the output. He positions talented people as the 20 percent who contribute the most.

8 For example, see Boudreau and Ramstead, 2007. Boudreau, J. W. and Ramstad, P. M., 2007. *Beyond HR: The new science of human capital*. Boston: Harvard Business Press.

9 For example, see the strengths research from Gallop, such as Rath, T. and Conchie, B., 2008. *Strengths based leadership: Great leaders, teams, and why people follow*. New York: Gallop Press.

10 Dweck, C., 2012. *Mindset: Changing the way you think to fulfil your potential*. London: Hachette UK.

11 For example, see Lepak, D. P. and Snell, S. A., 1999. The human resource architecture: Toward a theory of human capital allocation and development. *Academy of Management Review* 24(1), 31–48.

12 Silzer, R. and Church, A., 2010. Identifying and assessing high-potential talent: Current organizational practices. In: R. Silzer and B. Dowell, eds., *Strategy-driven talent management: A leadership imperative*. San Francisco: Jossey-Bass, 213–280.

13 Nijs, S., Gallardo-Gallardo, E., Dries, N. and Sels, L., 2014. A multidisciplinary review into the definition, operationalization, and measurement of talent. *Journal of World Business* 49(2), 180–191.

14 For more information, see https://dspace.lboro.ac.uk/dspace-jspui/bitstream/2134/27036/3/Thesis-2017-Evans.pdf (accessed 24.04.2019).

15 Slot, O., Timson, S. and Warr, C., 2017. *The talent lab: The secret to finding, creating and sustaining success*. London: Random House.

16 See Collings, D. G. and Mellahi, K., 2009. Strategic talent management: A review and research agenda. *Human Resource Management Review* 19(4), 304–313.

17 Scullion and Collings 2011:6. Global talent management: Introduction. In Scullion, H. and Collings, D., 2011. *Global talent management*. New York: Routledge.

18 For example, see Rotolo, C. T., Church, A. H., Adler, S., Smither, J. W., Colquitt, A. L., Shull, A. C., Paul, K. B. and Foster, G., 2018. Putting an end to bad talent management: A call to action for the field of industrial and organizational psychology. *Industrial and Organizational Psychology* 11(2), 176–219.

19 Collings (Collings, D. G., 2015. The contribution of talent management to organization success. In: K. Kraizer, J. Passmore, N. Rbelo dos Santos, S. Malvezzi, eds., *The Wiley Blackwell handbook of the psychology of training, development, and performance improvement*. Chichester, UK: Wiley) points to the lack of direct evidence linking talent to firm performance, which has been exacerbated by lack of consistent definitions and theoretical frameworks. Some evidence on high potential programmes suggests that 50 percent fail to strengthen talent pipelines and only 5 percent of High Potential programmes include appropriate follow-through. For a range of findings, see Tom Rose, PhD, 'Transforming high potential into high performance' www.trainingindustry.com/content/uploads/2017/08/Transforming-High-Potential-Into-High-Performance.pdf (accessed 05.06.2019). Collings was also keen to make the point that descriptions of benefits focus on the benefit for the organisation with little or no consideration of the benefits for other stakeholders. Collings, D. G., 2014. Toward mature talent management: Beyond shareholder value. *Human Resource Development Quarterly*, 25(3), 301–319.

20 Data presented by Bloomberg has a search facility. See www.bloomberg.com/graphics/ceo-pay-ratio/ for more information (accessed 30.04.2019). In the US, corporations are now required to publish pay differentials. Some, such as David Bolchover, challenge the idea that top-level pay is simply a matter of market forces. Instead they have pointed out

that lots of people have a vested interest in perpetuating the idea that the talent required to run a large corporation is very rare and should be rewarded (even if unsuccessful). Other markets have also seen such price inflation such as sport, with exceptionally high wages commanded by those at the top of their game.

21 This book provides strong evidence for the social impact of a scarcity mindset, be it of food, money, work or support. Mullainathan, S. and Shafir, E., 2013. *Scarcity: Why having too little means so much*. New York: Macmillan.

22 Rob Briner, 2015, www.hrmagazine.co.uk/article-details/whats-the-evidence-for-talent-management (accessed 24.04.2019).

23 Wiseman, L. and McKeown, G., 2010. *Multipliers: How the best leaders make everyone smarter*. New York: Harper Collins, is a highly practical book that expands these themes.

24 See the article www.managers.org.uk/insights/news/2017/november/the-three-personality-disorders-of-failed-ceos (accessed 30.04.2019).

25 Terms adopted by Frost, S. and Kalman, D. in their book, 2016. *Inclusive talent management: How business can thrive in an age of diversity*. London: Kogan Page.

26 For further information on disruptive talent, see www.oecam.com/the-oe/disruptive-talent/ (accessed 28.06.2019).

27 For example, see a Hogan Assessment thought piece, *The politics of potential: How organisational politics are poking holes in your high potential programme*, www.hoganassessments.com/thought-leadership/the-politics-of-potential/ (accessed 04.06.2019).

28 We readily attribute significant success (or failure) to the quality of the leader, hence the hero of the leader (and the significant number who are 'bailed out, booted or busted'). For more detail, see Meindl, J. R., Ehrlich, S. B. and Dukerich, J. M., 1985. The romance of leadership. *Administrative Science Quarterly*, 78–102.

29 How market leaders keep their edge. Treacy, M. and Wiersema, F., *Fortune* 31 (2) (2/6/95), 88, 6p, 4c.

30 Lawler III, E. E. and Boudreau, J. W., 2018. *Human resource excellence: An assessment of strategies and trends*. Redwood City, CA: Stanford University Press.

31 For example, Wilcox, H., 2016. *Effective talent management: Aligning strategy, people and performance*, New York: Routledge, devotes a whole chapter to exploring 'what sort of talent do we need?'

32 For more information, see www.bain.com/ (accessed 28.06.2019).

33 For example, see Charan, R., Barton, D. and Carey, D., 2018. *Talent wins: The new playbook for putting people first*. Boston: Harvard Business Press.

34 The nine-box grid is a widely used tool that puts people in one of nine boxes, according to their perceived talent on one axis and performance on the other. However, it has many critics due to its over-simplification and the focus on where to put people rather than what to do with that information. For a summary of the criticisms, see www.hrmagazine.co.uk/article-details/why-you-need-to-ditch-the-nine-box-grid (accessed 24.04.2019).

35 For example, David Collings, 2014. Toward mature talent management: Beyond shareholder value. (see above) and Sparrow, P., Scullion, H. and Tarique, I., 2014. *Strategic talent management: Contemporary issues in international context*. Cambridge: Cambridge University Press.

36 Garrow, V. and Hirsh, W., 2008. Talent management: Issues of focus and fit. *Public Personnel Management* 37(4), 389–402.

37 This is a consistent finding in research, for example, see Dries, N. and Peppermans, R., 2007. "Real" high-potential careers: An empirical study into the perspectives of organisations and high potentials. *Personnel Review* 37(1), 85–108. Or Thunnissen, M., 2016. Talent management for what, how and how well? An empirical exploration of talent management in practice. *Employee Relations* 38(1), 57–72.

38 Charan, Barton and Carey, 2018, *Talent wins: The new playbook for putting people first*. Boston: Harvard Business Review.

39 This has been found by many researchers. For example, see Dries, N. and De Gieter, S., 2014. Information asymmetry in high potential programs: A potential risk for psychological contract breach. *Personnel Review* 43(1), 136–162.

2 The future of work – talent required

Introduction

The changing workplace is a topic that interests people across many fields. Our intention here is not to compete with the excellent work of others, but to provide a summary of some of the themes that emerge across these varied sources. Footnotes will guide you to the source documents if you want to find out more. For this summary we've identified five key themes: the macrostructure of organisations; the internal structure of organisations; demographic changes; technological opportunities; and changes in career paths. In discussing these, we want to stress that we are describing them separately because it helps with presenting the information and thinking it through. However, as shown in Figure 2.1, the five themes inevitably interact such that changes in demography influence changes in structure and technology, changes in technology also influence changes in structures, and, in turn, changes in structures influence changes in technology. Similarly there are interactions between people's career paths and career expectations and the opportunities that are available to them as a result of macrostructures, internal structures, demographics and technology. In turn, the careers people want will create different resource opportunities and challenges for organisations.

Given that talent management is a strategic activity with largely long-term rather than short-term payback, it is essential that it is positioned in the context of the next wave of change. Therefore, having explored key trends and predictions for each theme, we then consider the implications of this for talent and career. This helps to establish how well the current talent models and approaches will adapt to these possible changes and help to drive competitive advantage. As you will see, our conclusion is that the current interpretation and implementation of talent management is ill-equipped to meet future needs as it is based on a set of assumptions about the workplace that seem to be no longer appropriate.

Predictions for the future of work

Macrostructure of organisations

We have borrowed the term *macrostructure* from sociology. It's a broad term that refers to the way society (or in our case, organisations across sectors and geographies) is structured in terms of relationships, dependencies and properties.

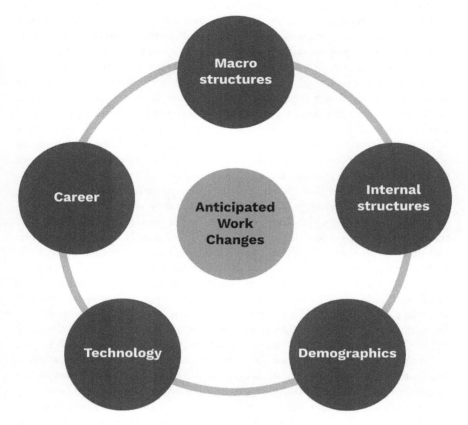

Figure 2.1 Anticipated workplace changes

The second half of the twentieth century and the early part of the twenty-first have seen ongoing amalgamation of businesses and domination by a few big players (think Google, Amazon, Netflix, 3M or General Electric). In the West, there has been growth in office-based work, service and distribution roles and a decline of roles in goods production. According to one recent report, added value service-based roles now make up nearly 80% of the US economy, with exports growing faster than any other sector.[1] However, in the midst of this growth of large business, new business models are emerging, which could provide insight into future changes.

Some of these new business models are based on facilitating direct contact between the service user and the service provider, sometimes referred to as the 'human cloud'[2] (e.g. Uber, fiverr, upwork, Airbnb and crowdsourcing platforms). They provide the flexibility that many organisations and individuals want to enable them to respond quickly to changing demands. Accurately understanding the growth in this type of organisational structure is difficult – by the nature of these businesses they don't publish annual reports for us to analyse. However, most would agree that the so-called 'gig economy' and the number of micro-enterprises are growing,[3] and some researchers predict that this will continue to grow, leading to a much smaller proportion of workers who will operate as employees with long-term, secure contracts.[4] This employment change represents a radical shift in the relationship between the employer and the worker. The psychological contract is fundamentally redrawn as the worker accepts less security and rights and accepts greater responsibility for keeping skills up-to-date and relevant. Similarly, it creates smaller discrete packages of work conducted by individuals who may not have any interest in the wider aims of the organisation they are working on behalf of. These individuals may be essential to the success of the organisation, or they may hold vital information, relationships and knowledge. But as things stand, some of them will not form part of the population that is included within the remit of talent management.

Another potential change has been described as new 'ecosystems'[5] of special-ist smaller businesses which emerge to provide the services and products that the large corporations find difficult to deliver. These may involve collaborations and alliances between a large number of niche organisations or individuals, each at the cutting edge of their field. These smaller, highly focused, entrepreneurial organisations provide a very different employment deal to their workers, often based on highly flexible ways of working and the opportunity to be involved in cutting-edge projects. This approach is already operating in some sectors, for example, crowdsourcing labs and the successful Procter & Gamble 'Connect + Develop'[6] initiative. This sources innovation partners rather than relying on the traditional model of internal (or fully acquired) research and development. Again, such business models leave bigger organisations relying on the expertise of talented people who lie outside its traditional organisational boundaries.

For talent management, this has wide-ranging implications. As indicated ear-lier, these changes challenge the typical boundaries of talent management, with strategically important people in strategically important roles situated outside the organisation. This requires consideration of the ways to interact and work together, for example, in terms of ongoing skills development and loyalty. It also requires a review of talent practices and how they should be adapted to apply to people who are not directly employed by the organisation.

Internal structures of organisations

Internal structures of organisations are continually evolving as leaders try to respond better to customer needs, to increase efficiency or to exploit new opportunities. As well as adapting the patterns and the boxes of reporting lines and roles, they also look at how to adapt the formal rules, processes, power, behaviours and sometimes the informal ones too. Over the years there have been different trends and solutions. There have been cycles of centralisation and decentralisation, of in-sourcing and outsourcing. Most organisations now oper-ate a form of matrix management to try to achieve the best of both worlds, with individual roles being clearly defined to support performance management, but also using dotted lines to encourage collaboration across functional and business unit lines. However, many structures still largely resemble a traditional hierarchy. Some claim that it is now time to challenge these structures and we now need to redefine the way in which people work together to achieve a common aim.

Many of the ideas for change stem from the application of complexity theory.[7] This encourages us to change our view of an organisation. Instead of seeing it as a machine to be managed and controlled, we are presented with the organisation as a complex adaptive system – one that, like the human brain or the internet, can manage itself without the need for hierarchy and one point of control. Over the years there have been examples of large and successful organisations turning their back on traditional hierarchies and finding new ways of doing things, for instance, Ricardo Semler's story of transforming the fortunes of Semco,[8] his family manufacturing business. The approach was radical. There were no set work hours, all employees voted on important decisions, people were encouraged to take a sabbatical to learn new skills, many employees set their own pay, there were few policies, and all corporate information was transparently shared with everyone.

More recently, Frederic Laloux[9] linked the evolution of organisations with advanced psychological development, describing different organisational structures by colours. Traditional organisations are termed as amber, with a focus on conforming. More developed organisations are categorised as orange (achievement) and then green (pluralistic). The most developed organisation is described as teal, with a clear purpose, the ability to self-organise and a safe space where people can connect and bring their whole self to work. Similarly, Mercer[10] describes these as 'molten structures', a way to respond to the need for plasticity with ongoing flattening and increasing emphasis on building networked communities (both internal and external). Some of these ideas are very radical and difficult to envisage, but there is growing interest.

Many of the principles of complexity and teal are recognised as a way in which organisations can achieve competitive advantage and be ready to respond quickly as the macrostructures around them change. Some of the principal differences of such an approach were summarised by Deloitte in their 2017 report on Global Human Capital Trends (see Table 2.1)[11] (Rewriting the rules for the digital age).

In our experience, many of these ideas are still at the experimental stage. However, we increasingly work with leaders who are interested in developing this thinking and are already experimenting with parts of it. For example, project-based structures, offices designed to promote conversation and collaboration, organisations offering a variety of work contracts and processes based on conversation rather than documentation. For these organisations, such new approaches create a need for a fundamentally different approach to talent management. As the organising principles shift from defined roles to projects, succession planning takes a different form and becomes more about deployment of skills than job title. As the work environment creates ongoing change, the nature, opportunities and purpose of personal development changes. As the role

Table 2.1 Deloitte summary of old rules and new rules for work

Old rules	New rules
Organised for efficiency and effectiveness	Organised for learning, innovation and customer impact
Company viewed as a hierarchy, with hierarchical decision rights, structure and leadership progression	Company viewed as an agile network, empowered by team leaders and fuelled by collaboration and knowledge-sharing
Structure based on business function with functional leaders and global functional groups	Structure based on work and projects, with teams focused on products, customers and services
Advancement through promotion upward with many levels to progress through	Advancement through many assignments, diverse experiences and multifunctional leadership assignments
People "become leaders" through promotion	People "create followers" to grow in influence and authority
Lead by direction	Lead by orchestration
Culture ruled by fear of failure and perceptions of others	Culture of safety, abundance and importance of risk-taking and innovation
Rules-based	Playbook-based
Roles and job titles clearly defined	Teams and responsibilities clearly defined, but roles and job titles change regularly
Process-based	Project-based

Source: Reproduced with permission: Josh Bersin, Bill Pelster, Jeff Schwarz, and Bernard Van der Vyver, "Introduction: Rewriting the rules for the digital age", *2017 Deloitte Global Human Capital Trends*, Deloitte Insights, February 28, 2017.

of the leader evolves, the skills, experiences and motivations of successful leaders will be different, requiring leaders who can rapidly help new teams to form and perform, who can bring out the best in people whatever the nature and form of their working relationship.

Demographic changes

According to an OECD report, projections for Japan illustrate the scale of the problem of falling birth-rates and aging population.[12] The Japanese government expects the country's overall population to decrease by 22–23% between 2010 and 2050, with people 65+ years accounting for 40% of the total. The 'elderly dependency ratio' (proportion of people aged 65+ to proportion of working-age people) is a particular concern and has risen across OECD countries in recent decades. This is likely to increase further as a result of longer lives. Alongside this is concern regarding population growth in developing nations. This is well illustrated by comparing the dependency ratio of Japan (45 in 2017) with that of India, a high growth nation (9 in 2017).[13] However, in line with trends observed as other nations develop, the rate of population growth in developing countries is declining as health, living conditions and education improvements are reflected in lower birth rates. For countries experiencing a declining population, the key challenges are to increase productivity, increase participation in the workplace beyond 65, encourage immigration of workers from other countries and find sustainable ways to fund and support older people. For the still-growing nations, the challenge is to increase education, job creation and political stability. For individuals worldwide, there are also significant questions about how to fund later life and the challenge of reconciling work-ability (literally the ability to do work) with increased life expectancy.[14]

All of these changes have a significant impact on the composition of the future workforce and therefore on the available talent. There are three particular issues we will briefly explore here: globalisation of the employment market, increasing work participation and generational differences. Increasing productivity offers additional ways to respond to changing demographics, but these will be explored alongside technical solutions later.

One response to these demographic changes is to see the workforce as global. This is already happening as organisations look to transfer work to places where there is a higher availability of qualified workers (with associated lower costs). Having started as 'off-shoring' (often in Asia or Eastern Europe), many organisations have reaped huge financial and talent benefits from broadening their talent market in these ways.[15] Growth in the availability of talented people from these locations is likely to continue, as illustrated by the statistic that if current trends continue, then by the 2020s, 40% of all young people with a degree will come from China and India.[16] Within many organisations there are also increasing efforts to look at resourcing requirements and deployment through a global rather than local lens. For example, if there is a need for a specialist skill, that skill can be searched for across the organisation rather than just within the local business unit or geography. Such a global resourcing model creates an internal job market place with an acceptance that the skills can lie anywhere in the organisation and virtual teams are an appropriate delivery mechanism. The global skills and talent challenge is complex and paradoxical. On one hand, there is the global phenomenon of graduate underemployment. On the other hand, there is the repeated complaint from business that there is a shortage of suitable individuals for leadership positions and a shortage of technological talent. Many countries wish to reduce the reliance on expatriates to fill senior positions and develop more 'local' talent. Meanwhile, other countries experience 'brain drain' as highly educated individuals seek more lucrative positions overseas. Nevertheless the global homogeneity of business systems, the prevalence of English as a global business language and rising education levels have caused a radical shift. Jobs in the so-called 'knowledge based economy' are moving to where labour costs are lower. In organisational talent terms, this can create challenges in global succession planning and the development of professional skills.[17]

Demographic changes are also stimulating us to rethink what we mean by our 'working life'. In many countries, government policy is contributing to this as state retirement ages increase in response to unsustainable financial models of state retirement benefits, with the consequence that working lives become longer. Many of these issues are brought together in a fascinating book by Lynda Gratton and Andrew Scott of London Business School.[18] They suggest that these demographic changes require us to shift our mindset of the normal stages of life. For generations, the expectation has been three key stages: education, work and retirement. However, with a longer, healthier life and smaller working population, we will need to think more in terms of multiple cycles of education, work and other things (which may include greater leisure or caring or community-based work). For the workplace this necessitates a significant change in how we think about career, engagement and the relationship between age and seniority. For example, it could be that apprentices in their 50s train alongside those in their 20s. We need to think how to motivate and engage people over a working life that extends into their 70s. Equally it creates opportunities for new approaches to remuneration, for example, the opportunity to fund a 'learning pot' rather than a 'pension pot', as has been the case in Singapore with 'Skillsfuture'.[19]

Further workplace challenges could result from what are believed to be differences in motivations of the millennial generation. It is often suggested that millennials are looking for a different career deal, expecting a greater sense of purpose, a desire for learning, treatment as an individual, more rapid progression and regular positive reinforcement or feedback.[20] However, research evidence to support this is modest, and perhaps the biggest message here is the desire for individual treatment and meaning, which would seem to be increasingly valued by people of all generations.[21]

Technological opportunities

We are all aware that technology is dramatically changing the way we work, often referred to as the 'Fourth Industrial Revolution'.[22] To repeat the much quoted phrase from *Shift Happens*,[23] 'we are currently preparing students for jobs that don't yet exist, using technologies that haven't been invented, in order to solve problems we don't yet realise are problems'. More specific data also reinforce this view. For example, by 2020, smart cities will include 9.7 billion connected things, an increase from 1.1 billion in 2015, and driverless cars could free up 50 billion hours each year in the United States (a potential employment issue given that 40% of US males are currently employed in driving-based occupations).[24] There are bound to be many consequences of technological change, some bringing considerable ethical considerations. Rather than taking a broad look at these implications, in this section we will focus on two areas of particular relevance for the talent agenda: firstly the impact of technology on the skills that are needed and secondly the workplace opportunities arising from technology in terms of learning, collaboration and engagement.

The impact of technology on the nature of jobs is likely to be driven by the uptake of new technologies. A 2018 paper by PwC[25] suggests three waves of automation. Wave one, the algorithmic wave (to the early 2020s) is predicted to be largely about automation of processes and analysis of structured data.

This is anticipated to impact most on data-driven sectors including financial services. The second wave (to the late 2020s) is seen as being dominated by augmentation, with greater use of technology to support decision making and increased use in moving objects from place to place (such as in warehouses and airports). The third wave is seen as the autonomous wave (to the mid-2030s) with technological advances meaning that jobs requiring physical dexterity can be completed through robotics and that AI can take over problem-solving tasks in more complex situations.

The human impact of such advances were reviewed in a report commissioned by the UK's CIPD (Chartered Institute of Personnel and Development, the professional body for HR),[26] who concluded that technology would complement human skills, potentially removing mundane aspects of roles to enable more 'human work' and emotional interaction to take place. The view that 'human skills' will remain in demand is supported by the Mercer 2018 study on Global Talent Trends. Thus, in talent terms, we need to consider where human skills will add unique value that cannot readily be replicated by technology. These are the skills we will particularly need in our organisations of the future.

A second skill impact of technological advances is also made by both the CIPD research and the Mercer 2018 study. For these technologies to be developed and implemented, workers with deep technological expertise will be required. Workers who can rapidly adapt and learn new technologies and find ways to exploit them will be needed. Equally, all workers will need to be skilled at working with new and evolving technologies. Without this, uptake of technological solutions is likely to be hindered. In the context of talent, these points challenge both the roles people do and our current way of assessing people. For example, the HR function will need to be redefined as the compliance aspects of the work become increasingly automated. In recruitment, expecting a certain number of years' experience may no longer be relevant due to the decreasing half-life of technology and knowledge. Rather, the key skill will be the ability to learn, adapt and harness the power of a range of new technologies and to use them legally and ethically. These changes will apply to all people working with the organisation, be they employed or contracted, and in any of the four talent quadrants.

In addition to changing the nature of jobs and skills requirements, technology is likely to have a growing impact on learning, assessment and engagement. Comprehensive learning management systems (LMS) are now starting to realise the dreams of the early e-learning pioneers as bite-sized, relevant learning becomes available to employees via mobile, interactive apps.[27] Learning is also increasingly accessible with Massive Open On-line Courses (MOOCs) expanding (according to some data having over 80 million students enrolled)[28] and world-class events available to watch via TED talks and YouTube. This creates both benefits and challenges as employers try to understand the comparative value of traditional learning, MOOCs and self-learning. Technology has a role to play in assessment with increasing use of online and innovative tools such as gamification, AI evaluation of interview data and e-tray exercises.[29] Social media are also increasingly being used to reinforce employee branding as a tool to attract and engage talented employees. Utilising models and techniques from product marketing, such approaches are becoming progressively more sophisticated, especially to attract 'passive' candidates who are not actively job hunting.[30] Technological advances also make it easier to achieve the global collaboration that was explored as part of the changing macro and internal structures. For example, LinkedIn supports leaders and organisations in quickly identifying internal or external candidates with the skills or experience being sought.

All of these aspects of technology are likely to influence the future of talent management. Technological advances will create demand for different skills and experiences. They will also create opportunities for new ways of delivering the talent agenda.

Changes in career paths

Career is a commonly used term, often applied in quite a narrow way, traditionally referring to someone's hierarchical progression within a particular profession. However, within the academic literature, career is considered in broader terms as the way work is experienced over the course of a working life.[31] This relates not just to objective measures of career success (such as job title, salary and promotion history) but also to subjective measures (such as satisfaction, meaning and thriving).[32] Taking this wider description of career, it is easy to see how the structural, technological and demographic changes described earlier will create some fundamental changes in the way careers are experienced. Indeed changes in career have long been heralded with talk of the death of organisational careers, with people freely moving between roles.[33] In this section we explore two additional themes that are pertinent to talent and career: what people want from their career and the role of career self-management.

Will changes in the nature of work change what people want from their career? Research to date has suggested that despite the changing structures of employment, most people continue to think of careers as organisationally based.[34] Some suggest that new forms of career are now possible, combining some of the freedom, flexibility and empowerment of an individually driven career with the benefits of continuity, meaning and relationships that can emerge from being part of an organisation.[35] Others have taken this further, indicating that there needs to be a fundamental shift in the employee value proposition:[36] It is suggested that this needs to move from a loyalty or engagement contract to a 'thrive contract'. This moves attention from meeting the employee's needs for achievement, relationships and fairness to an environment that prioritises purpose, meaning and impact with joint career ownership and ongoing learning. This was summarised in a recent PwC report as the importance of helping people to thrive in order to deliver strong business performance.[37] They proposed that organisations need to focus more on the employee experience and embrace modern career paths that provide multiple routes to meet diverse individual needs (rather than the historic 'up or out' mindset). Common to much of the thinking on the future of career is the need to individualise, to recognise that people have different wants, needs and aspirations at different stages in their working lives. However, it may be naïve to have such aspirations for the development of thriving at work. A recent book by David Graeber[38] suggests that half of all jobs are pointless, and the proportion seems to be increasing. This creates inefficiency for the organisations and has a damaging psychological impact on people doing jobs that they can see are meaningless.

The second theme that emerges in career is the increasing focus on the individual as responsible for 'owning' their career. Our research shows that the idea of individual accountability is widely accepted by HR leaders and individuals. However, many people report that they don't know what this means in practice or how they can be proactive in developing their career within their own work context. Whilst some organisations are helping them (see Chapter 5 for examples), there tends to be a lack of information and support. The need for comprehensive information and support is also recognised by governments and policy makers who are keen to support individuals to be able to proactively manage their careers.[39] This is likely to become increasingly important with the work changes described earlier. There is a particular risk that people with low social capital[40] could find it difficult to find employment without career management skills. Indeed the European-funded ACUMEN project[41] has emphasised the importance of career management skills by describing them as the 'new literacy'.

Implications of these changes for talent management

The previous sections have, we hope, provided a helpful overview of some current and anticipated changes in the world of work. Many of the points we have raised will have significant implications for talent management. We have signposted some of these along the way and have now summarised them in Table 2.2.

Table 2.2 Implications of work changes for talent management

Change	Potential implications for talent management
Macrostructures	• Strategically critical skills and knowledge may lie outside organisational boundaries but need to be considered as part of the talent strategy. • Changes in the psychological contract are likely to impact on mutual commitment between employer and employee; established ways to engage and develop talented people will need to be reviewed. • Historical talent management success measures such as succession planning, retention, engagement, internal development and promotions may no longer be appropriate.

(*Continued*)

Table 2.2 (Continued)

Change	Potential implications for talent management
Internal structures	• Larger organisations will have a myriad of possible career pathways as there are fewer hierarchies and more project-based work; career development will need to be reappraised. • Global resourcing models make geographic location less relevant for larger organisations and open new opportunities for smaller organisations to consider. • Lifelong learning will have increasing importance, and learning agility will become a key capability, as does the ability to effectively collaborate, indicating new selection, development and performance management criteria.
Technical opportunities	• New specialisms will quickly evolve and command high market demand/price; organisations with access to these skills are likely to have competitive advantage, so early identification of needs and development of skills will become more critical. • Many businesses will depend on quick adoption, so workers who can quickly adapt and implement new technology will be in demand. • Joined-up thinking will be required with governments and educators in respect of skills and developing future labour supply and accessible retraining. • Technology will provide new opportunities for learning, attraction and engagement, but will require ongoing investment.
Demographic	• Generational integration will occur as people go through career stages at different ages and may require a change in expectations and selection criteria for different roles (such as apprenticeships). • Longer working life indicates a need to find ways to fund learning and retraining throughout employment. • Changes in geographical availability of talent with possible rising costs in developing markets suggest a need to constantly review availability and location of people with different skills.
Career pathways	• Increase in career self-management may disadvantage some people. Organisations may benefit from supporting individuals to manage their employability and career transitions. • Changing perceptions of career suggests the importance of understanding what our talented workers want from their work and providing greater flexibility. • Variety of career opportunities indicates the importance of developing new relationships with all workers (employees or others engaged in strategically important work), offering a clear employer value proposition and moving towards thriving.

Our summary indicates that it is time to reflect on talent management and how the approach may need to evolve to meet these predicted changes. When this is combined with the concerns raised in the previous chapter, the case for change becomes even more compelling. The previous predictions suggest that if we retain our current approaches, the scarcity mindset will be reinforced as the availability of 'ready now' 'traditionally employed' talent is likely to reduce. The changes also indicate that reliance on individual heroes will impede an organisation's ability to evolve and harness the power of self-managed teams. A dependence on formal process is also likely to reduce the ability to flex and quickly address emerging talent needs in innovative ways that respond to unique circumstances. Similarly, anchoring talent processes in historic assessments of what is needed is unlikely to deliver competitive advantage. Finally the future of work clearly suggests the need to respond to what the individual wants and to find a way to work in partnership, helping people to thrive and find the motivation which will drive their talent.

Reflections

In this chapter, we have introduced five themes to explore how the world of work seems to be changing. We have illustrated how these are likely to impact on the way talent management is approached if organisations want to retain competitive advantage. We have shown how these themes could magnify some of the challenges of talent management which we introduced in Chapter 1. This substantiates our view that talent management as it is currently practised is not fit for purpose in the short term and is likely to become even less effective in the future.

You may find the following questions helpful as you reflect on how changes in the workplace may impact on your future talent needs.

- What work changes have you observed over the past five years?
- What changes do you anticipate over the next five years?
- How could the changes in macrostructures change the key functions carried out by your organisation?
- What are the likely and possible changes to internal structures?
- Which demographic trends are most likely to impact your business in the next five years?
- What technical changes do you anticipate, and what are the hard-to-replicate 'human' skills that you may need?
- How do you think the requirements and expectations of the people who work in your organisation will change?
- How do you see these things impacting on your talent needs?
- Who else in your organisation is thinking about these implications?

Notes

1 Deloitte report https://www2.deloitte.com/content/dam/insights/us/articles/4674_IbtN-July-2018/DI_IbtN-July-2018.pdf (accessed 13.06.2019).

2 For example, see Schwab, K., 2017. *The fourth industrial revolution*. London: Penguin Random House.

3 Information from the Gig Economy Data Hub, a partnership between the ILR School at Cornell University and the Future of Work Initiative, www.gigeconomydata.org/ (accessed 13.06.2019). We are also aware that some of these changes have consistently been predicted for the past thirty years and have yet to materialise to the extent that was anticipated.

4 E.g. UK Commission for Employment and Skills report 'The Future of Work Jobs and Skills in 2030 https://assets.publishing.service.gov.uk/government/uploads/system/uploads/attachment_data/file/303335/the_future_of_work_key_findings_edit.pdf (accessed 13.06.2019).

5 Gratton, L and Scott, A., 2016. *The 100 year Life: Living and working in an age of longevity*. London: Bloomsbury.

6 www.pgconnectdevelop.com/what-is-connect-develop/ (accessed 13.06.2019).

7 For a short introduction to complexity theory, we suggest the following video www.youtube.com/watch?v=i-ladOjo1QA (accessed 28.06.2019).

8 See Semler, R., 1993. *Maverick*. New York: Warner Books.

9 Laloux, F., 2014. *Reinventing organizations: A guide to creating organizations inspired by the next stage in human consciousness*. Nelson Parker.

10 www.mercer.com/our-thinking/career/voice-on-talent/people-first-mercers-2018-global-talent-trends-study.html (accessed 28.06.2018).

11 Deloitte in their 2017 report on Global Human Capital Trends (Rewriting the rules for the digital age), https://www2.deloitte.com/cn/en/pages/human-capital/articles/global-human-capital-trends-2017.html (accessed 13.06.2019).

12 http://oecdinsights.org/2016/04/11/the-case-of-the-shrinking-country-japans-demographic-and-policy-challenges-in-5-charts/ shows the particular challenges facing Japan and suggests that Japan illustrates the problems that will be faced by other OECD countries in future years (accessed 13.06.2019).

13 For a full list by nation, visit https://data.worldbank.org/indicator/SP.POP.DPND.OL (accessed 13.06.2019).

14 For some early research on this, see Nielsen, J., 1999. Employability and workability among Danish employees. *Experimental Aging Research* 25(4), 393–397.

15 A systematic literature review illustrated strong evidence for the benefits of offshoring in technology and indicated that it is a trend that is likely to continue Strasser, A.R.T.U.R. and Westner, M.A.R.K.U.S., 2015. Information systems offshoring: Results of a systematic literature review. *Journal of Information Technology Management* 26(2), 70–142.

16 Deloitte report https://www2.deloitte.com/content/dam/insights/us/articles/4674_IbtN-July-2018/DI_IbtN-July-2018.pdf (accessed 13.06.2019).

17 Rothwell, A., Herbert, I. and Seal, W., 2011. Shared service centres and professional employability. *Journal of Vocational Behavior* 79, 241–252.

18 Gratton, L., Scott, A. and Caulkin, S., 2016. 100 year life: A gift or a curse. *London Business School Review* 27(2), 40–43.

19 For more information, visit www.skillsfuture.sg/credit (accessed 24.04.2019).

20 Adkins, A. and Rigoni, B., 2016. Millennials want jobs to be development opportunities. *Gallop Business Journal*. https://www.gallup.com/workplace/236438/millennials-jobs-development-opportunities.aspx (accessed 20.08.2019).

21 For example, see Duffy, R. D., Autin, K. L. and Bott, E. M., 2015. Work volition and job satisfaction: Examining the role of work meaning and person – environment fit. *The Career Development Quarterly* 63(2), 126–140.

22 Schwab, 2017.

23 Shift happens first appeared in 2006. Planned as content for a staff development day by Karl Fisch, of Arapahoe High School in the USA, it has been published and modified by manner under a Creative Commons licence. It poses challenging questions about the future nature of work and the role of education.

24 EY report, 2016. The upside of disruption: Megatrends shaping 2016 and beyond, www.ey.com/gl/en/issues/business-environment/ey-megatrends (accessed 13.06.2019).

25 PwC 2018. Will robots really steal our jobs: An international analysis of the potential long term impact of automation, www.pwc.co.uk/economic-services/assets/international-impact-of-automation-feb-2018.pdf (accessed 13.06.2019).

26 The report was based on a 'rapid evidence review', conducted by our Loughborough colleagues Professor Hislop, D., Dr Coombs, C., Dr Taneva, S. and Dr Barnard, S., December 2017. *Impact of artificial intelligence, robotics and automation technologies on work*. CIPD.

27 For an example of how this works in practice, visit the customer stories via the Fuse website, https://fuse.fuseuniversal.com/communities/2086 (accessed 13.06.2019).

28 For example, see www.class-central.com/report/mooc-stats-2017/ (accessed 13.06.2019).

29 For examples of these see Arctic Shores, see www.arcticshores.com/; Hirevue www.hirevue.com/ (accessed 13.06.2019).

30 SHRM survey on 'Using Social Media for Talent Acquisition – recruitment and screening' 2015 www.shrm.org/hr-today/trends-and-forecasting/research-and-surveys/Documents/SHRM-Social-Media-Recruiting-Screening-2015.pdf (accessed 13.06.2019).

31 For example, see Arthur and Rousseau define career as '*the unfolding sequence of a person's work experiences over time*', Arthur, M. B. and Rousseau, D. M., 1996. *The boundaryless career.* Oxford: Oxford University Press.

32 For more information on thriving at work, see chapter seven.

33 For example, the idea of the 'boundaryless career' (Arthur and Rousseau, 1996). However, these changes have not yet had as much impact as predicted. For example, see Clarke, M., 2013. The organizational career: Not dead but in need of redefinition. *The International Journal of Human Resource Management* 24(4), 684–703.

34 For example, see Dries, N., 2011. The meaning of career success: Avoiding reification through a closer inspection of historical, cultural, and ideological contexts. *Career Development International* 16(4), 364–384.

35 For example, Clarke has described five propositions of a 'new organisational career', Clarke, 2013.

36 See the Mercr Global Talent Trends 2018 report. This can be downloaded from www.mmc.com/insights/publications/2018/jan/mercer-global-talent-trends-2018.html (accessed 26.04.2019).

37 To download the report, visit www.pwc.com/gx/en/people-organisation/pdf/pwc-preparing-for-tomorrows-workforce-today.pdf (accessed 26.04.2019).

38 Graeber, D., 2019. *Bullshit jobs: The rise of pointless work, and what we can do about it.* London: Penguin Books Ltd.

39 For example, see the research conducted within the EU by ACUMEN www.acumen.website/en/home/ (accessed 26.04.2019).

40 High social capital enables people to draw on the resources of others through strong networking and interpersonal skills. High social capital has been linked with high career success. For further information, see Adler, P. S. and Kwon, S. W., 2002. Social capital: Prospects for a new concept. *Academy of management review* 27(1), 17–40.

41 See endnote 38.

3 Talent liberation – a new metaphor

Introduction

We've provided evidence to suggest that talent management as it's generally practised is not fit for purpose in the current world of work. Furthermore, we've seen that future work changes are likely to exacerbate this – making the current approaches even less suitable. So how do we approach the challenge of ensuring the 'best people' are in the 'most strategic roles'? How can organisations better understand the short- and long-term talent risks they face? How can we think of talent management in new and different ways to help us to find better solutions? How can we harness more of people's talent and help them to operate at their Personal Best? How can we identify and develop people with High Potential? How can we help individuals to thrive?

In this chapter, we introduce 'talent liberation' as a different way of approaching the current talent challenges being faced by organisations. Drawing on approaches in the fields of innovation and creativity, we show how adopting this metaphor instead of the commonly used 'talent war' can change our perception of the problem.[1] This changed perception can result in very different ways of framing the challenges, opening possibilities for more creative solutions. We propose that the very label of 'talent management' contributes to the challenges we have discussed so far. The word 'management' carries clear connotations of control and order. This anchors us to a worldview where organisations change as a result of controlled and intentional interventions which produce predictable results. Based on this, current approaches with their tools, techniques and processes make perfect sense in the quest for achieving best practice. Indeed this is the dominant way of looking at organisations, viewed as pragmatic and obvious – and thus rarely questioned.[2] However, whilst helpful in businesses which operate in stable environments, this worldview does not translate well to the knowledge economy[3] and does not help us to answer the questions posed earlier. We therefore propose that 'liberation' is a more fitting representation of our intentions, symbolising the opportunity to set talent free rather than to manage, control and potentially constrict it.

In describing what we mean by talent liberation, we will draw on wide-ranging literature and perspectives, including agile methodologies, systems thinking and complexity theory. We will start by drawing some parallels between talent liberation and the widely used 'agile' approaches. We will then introduce five premises of talent liberation that address the talent management challenges described in Chapter 1 and the changes in the world of work described in Chapter 2. This approach to talent does not change the definitions of talent as Personal Best, High Potential, Strengths and Gifted. Nor does this approach discount the different talent strategies commonly adopted (as outlined in Chapter 1). However, it does fundamentally change the way talent management is viewed and the way that talented people are utilised within an organisation. The outcome from this can be to maximise existing talent, build agility, grow engagement and increase capability through an approach based on partnership among all of the stakeholders. We're not claiming to have all the answers, and we're not claiming that it's perfect. What we are claiming is that despite lots of effort, the current approaches aren't working well. So if we want to reach some workable solutions, we need to look at the problem in new ways.

In doing this, we have been inspired by the 'The Manifesto for Agile Software Development'.[4]

The start of Agile . . .

Imagine starting a movement while on a ski trip . . . in February 2001 a group of seventeen friends, colleagues and competitors from the world of IT had a couple of days at the Snowbird ski resort (Wasatch Mountains in Utah). They sought an alternative approach – away from the documentation and process-driven approaches to software development that dominated. Alongside relaxing, skiing and talking, they found common ground and wrote it as a 'Manifesto for Agile Software Development'. As the 'Agile Alliance', they have role-modelled collaboration and openness, sharing ideas and inviting people to join them. What they brought together has created a fundamental shift in the way projects are 'managed'.

Agile is not anti-methodology; rather it embraces methodology and process – but in a way that is practical and generates learning rather than pretty charts for their own sake. The approach is all about finding better ways, underpinned by learning, and building this learning into everything. In doing this, they are aware that a lot of agile is about people and culture. They value:

Individuals and interactions over processes and tools
Working software over comprehensive documentation
Customer collaboration over contract negotiation
Responding to change over following a plan

This is backed up by 12 principles, which can be found on their manifesto site.

The desire for agile software development was born out of frustration with the prevailing approaches. The originators saw that the received wisdom about developing software with detailed up-front planning was flawed when conditions changed. This was a problem, as projects were increasingly dynamic, with frequent changes in goals, resources and stakeholders. Since the start of the century, agile has become a global movement with an emphasis on conversations, collaboration and responsiveness.[5] As agile has become more widely known, it has been applied to new spheres, including HR. Some of this thinking has been brought together by key HR influencers (such as Josh Bersin and David Rock) as an Agile HR Manifesto,[6] which is supported by five principles of agile HR. This is often applied to elements of the HR agenda without necessarily implementing change across the function. For example, in many organisations, annual appraisals have been replaced by a more flexible and agile 'check-in' approach, and learning is moving to be more 'on-demand'. However, other processes (such as succession planning) remain on a set annual cycle, driven by process, documentation and a defined timetable.[7]

Manifesto for Agile HR development

We are uncovering better ways of developing an engaging workplace culture by doing it and helping others do it.
  Through this work we have come to value:

Collaborative networks over hierarchical structures
Transparency over secrecy
Adaptability over prescriptiveness
Inspiration and engagement over management and retention
Intrinsic motivation over extrinsic rewards
Ambition over obligation

That is, while there is value in the items on the right, we value the items on the left more.

© 2001, the Agile Manifesto authors[8]

Five premises of talent liberation

Talent Liberation cannot claim to have been born in a ski chalet in Utah (regrettably). However, there are other parallels. Our starting point is that the current approaches aren't working and seem to lack the flexibility needed in an increasingly dynamic and changing environment. In developing our thinking, we have engaged with others who are equally dissatisfied with the current state of play of talent management. In our conversations and collaborations, we have come to many of the same conclusions as the agile pioneers in Utah and the thinkers behind the Agile HR Manifesto. They summarised things that they valued over the traditional approaches. In a similar way, we have taken our list of five problems with talent management described in Chapter 1 and positioned five corresponding premises of talent liberation (see Table 3.1).

When we talk with people about these five premises, they nod their heads. These seem to be sensible statements that are easy to accept. However, based on the dominance of other approaches, it would appear that these premises are not so easy to act on. We will now get under the skin of what we mean by these statements, exploring the evidence and the potential implications for how to approach talent within organisations. In the following chapters, we shall then move on to practical ways in which these premises can be applied to liberate more talent within your organisation.

Table 3.1 Five premises of talent liberation

Talent challenges	Premise of talent liberation
Mindset of scarcity	1. **Talent is not as scarce as we think**. 'Ready now' talent may be in short supply, but there are lots of people with the 'raw materials', fitting into the Personal Best, Personal Strengths and High Potential descriptions of talent. We need to be better at finding ways to tap into this.
Cult of individual hero	2. **High performance is a result of teams as well as individuals**. Sustainable high performance is achieved through talented teams, as well as strong individuals. Both are important to create and grow competitive advantage.
Lack of strategic clarity	3. **We need to be responsive to changing talent needs. Future business needs may change**. To be ready to respond to these, we need to prepare for a range of scenarios by having access to a diversity of skills, experiences and behaviour and being willing to access these in different ways.
Dominance of formal process	4. **Formal processes are only part of the answer**. Formal elements of talent management tend to be bureaucratic and inflexible. They need to be balanced by support for informal approaches and a culture which encourages developing and engaging talent, allowing solutions to emerge.
Missing half the story	5. **Success depends on partnership between the organisation and the people**. Motivation is a key component of performance. Therefore, any approach to talent needs to address this, finding common ground between individual and organisation rather than everything just for the benefit of the organisation.

Talent is not as scarce as we think

In September 1865, Elizabeth Garrett Anderson was the first woman to pass her UK medical exams. By 1911, there were still only 495 women on the Medical Register in Britain. As of November 2018, this had changed to more than 137,000 registered female UK doctors, representing 47% of the total. The percentage of female doctors is continuing to increase. Within the 30–34 age group, 57% of doctors are female.[9]

We suggest that this dramatic increase (repeated worldwide across many professions) has little to do with a sudden increase in the innate abilities of women. Rather we contend that the social and educational experiences of women now enable them to develop their skills to become medics. Data produced by the World Economic Forum[10] provide a global breakdown of gender parity across health, education, the economy and politics. This shows that women entering employment now typically have the same level of education as men. However, progress towards equality in the other areas is slow, particularly in countries which are not creating an environment that is conducive to increasing female participation. The report also focuses on the lack of female participation in STEM subjects (30% of all male graduates have studied STEM subjects compared to just 16% of female graduates), suggesting that increasing female participation in STEM subjects will be crucial to meet the skills needs of 'the fourth industrial revolution'.

There is plenty of evidence that women remain an under-recognised and consequently untapped source of talent. Evidence suggests that there are many other groups whose abilities are not being utilised. For example, the shocking data on the accelerating 'racial wealth divide' in the USA[11] illustrate the economic and social consequences of wealth differences between people of Black, Latino and White groups. The lower wealth of the Black and Latino groups is seen as having a number of consequences, including reduced participation in tertiary education, which in turn reduces the availability of talent. To counter this, a recent global conference on 'untapped talent' advocated using technology-enabled assessments to overcome bias. This could create new ways to identify people's talent and to collect evidence of people's ability to learn. This, they argue, has the potential to broaden the visible talent pool, particularly to address the current STEM shortages and to create greater fairness.[12]

Liberating some of this talent requires intervention by governments to provide educational opportunities that enable everyone to develop their strengths regardless of social or ethnic background. At present there seems to be a lack of effective political action, and these issues are pressing. Therefore, whilst there may be opportunities to lobby government, our focus in this book is on what you can do at an organisational level.

Taking a talent liberation perspective, we suggest that there are three sources of untapped talent which can help you to challenge the mindset of scarcity:

- *Spotting the 'High Potential' talented people who could be hidden.* This is a readily available source of talented people if you can locate and develop them. Some research has suggested that typical ways of identifying the 'top talent' (such as leadership) may miss between 60 and 75% of the talented people who exist.[13] That's a lot of people who aren't visible and could be used to contribute in different ways to the organisation's success.[14]
- *Increasing everyone's 'Personal Best'.* Through systematic development it is possible to increase the mean level of performance. As we saw in Chapter 1, who counts as 'talent' is not fixed, and levels of performance across many fields are constantly improving. So if your organisation can improve your mean level of performance before others, you will gain a competitive advantage.
- *Identifying new sources of 'ready now' talented people (Gifted, High Potential, Personal Best or Personal Strengths).* These people have the skills, experiences and behaviours you need, but aren't being attracted to work with you. These people may be attracted by different working models such as interim or contract, or they may be attracted by a different recruitment approach that emphasises the strengths and characteristics you seek rather than the experiences.[15]

With the right actions and nurturing, these three approaches can help you to identify and access new supplies of talented people, tailored to meet the needs of the organisation. Aligned with this, there is growing interest in supporting people to apply a 'growth mindset'[16] so that they are open to new learning experiences and constantly looking for ways to improve, seeing failure as a learning opportunity rather than confirmation that they do not have the ability. Furthermore, providing these growth opportunities creates more fulfilling work and careers, potentially enabling people to thrive, increasing engagement and retention and thus further increasing your supply of talented people.

High performance is a result of teams as well as individuals

In May 2016, an inspiring story captivated the world. It was a story that illustrated the power of the team over the power of the individual. Leicester City, 5000–1 outsiders, had just won the English Premier Football League. Their squad had cost less than half that of the rest of the top five, and their wage bill was similarly far lower[17] and less than a quarter of some of the top teams. Yet they had won. With no high-profile talent or cult of the individual megastar, they were described as a group of outsiders.[18] The difference? The ability to spot talented players early and create an environment in which they could flourish played its part. So too did the team spirit developed by the manager, Claudio Ranieri, and also the supportive family atmosphere created by the late owner, Vichai Srivaddhanaprabha. The contribution of the team on and off the pitch all contributed to the success.

In business, as in football, there can be an assumption that if you spend enough on the 'best' talent, the results will follow. This has led many organisations we speak with to take a 'people' approach to talent management, becoming preoccupied with finding highly talented individual leaders, those who fit the 'Gifted' description of talent. Certainly there is an attractive simplicity to the view of cause and effect that the best leader will cause the best performance. However, as we saw in Chapter 1, the so-called 'top leaders' do not guarantee top performance.[19] Moreover, the emphasis on the individual tends to overshadow the influence of team and context. Jeffery Pfeffer made a compelling case for this in his 2001 paper, 'Fighting the war for talent is hazardous to your organisation's health'.[20] He pointed out that effective teams often outperform talented collections of individuals, an observation that is frequently visible on sports fields around the world.[21] Perhaps this focus on the individual is convenient. It tends to be easier to look at changing an individual rather than trying to address the complexity of culture, decision making and other enablers of performance.

Including team as an important element of performance is consistent with the anticipated work changes described in Chapter 2. It also ensures a source of competitive advantage that is harder to replicate than recruiting a talented individual who could be poached by a competitor. This idea is well articulated in the Resource-Based View of strategy.[22] This suggests that competitive advantage is situated in the history, culture, skills and practices of the organisation and therefore not in the gift of an individual leader. Similarly, the research on High Performance Work Systems[23] indicates that high performance does not automatically result from an individual's high skills or abilities. Rather it is suggested that discretionary effort and improved performance are influenced by three types of practices: those that develop skills, those that increase motivation and those that provide opportunities for people to contribute and use their abilities. (This is sometimes referred to as AMO: Abilities, Motivation and Opportunities.) These three elements of performance (ability, motivation and opportunity) are in turn influenced by teamwork and the working environment and culture[24] (to be explored later).

Despite the recognised importance of teams, there is little crossover of ideas in the research and literature between talent and team.[25] However, taking a talent liberation perspective, we suggest that the focus of talent should broaden to include the contribution and performance of team as well as individuals and the interplay between them.[26] Questions to consider include: how do leaders support the growth of teams as well as individuals? How is the contribution, performance and potential of teams recognised and valued? How are teams encouraged to share learning and to collaborate across boundaries? Whilst a detailed review of the mechanics of team performance is beyond the scope of this book, we do expand the scope of talent discussions to include elements of the team.

We need to be responsive to changing talent needs

New and critically important jobs are emerging. According to *Forbes*,[27] one of the hardest-to-fill vacancies in 2017 was a 'Data Scientist'. Another was 'Information Security Analyst'. Ten years ago, few (if any) organisations would have identified these roles in their talent strategy. Similarly, the World Economic Forum in 2016 listed 10 jobs that didn't exist 10 years previously. This included 'App developer', 'Social Media Manager' and 'Drone Operators'. What new, critically important roles will emerge in the next 10 years?

As we saw in Chapter 1, it is challenging for leaders to define a detailed long-term strategy which makes it difficult to identify future talent requirements. Furthermore, the changes in the world of work described in Chapter 2 impact on the environment within which a talent strategy is enacted. Responding to such a high level of change creates difficulties in developing any strategies, particularly people-based strategies such as talent management, which tend to operate based on long-term returns. It would seem, therefore, that rather than try to adapt or hold on to current approaches, we need to embrace the challenge and find ways of developing talent strategies that enhance the organisation's ability to perform in an uncertain and changing world.

This more agile approach would be based on exploring possible scenarios, managing risk and being highly responsive, with a variety of talented people with differing skill sets ready and available. Some of these skills may not be needed, so people with these skills would need to be retrained, redeveloped or redeployed. For example, succession planning would focus on understanding the talent implications of possible future scenarios and taking action to minimise risk rather than the current preoccupation with analysing the gap between a set view of current and future capability requirements.[28] Our conversations with CEOs suggest that this is what they want. They want to engage in conversations about how to maximise future flexibility, to explore a range of strategic scenarios to understand the type of skills, experiences, behaviours and motivations that will contribute to organisational success.

There is a challenge to taking scenario-based, risk approaches. Whilst they make logical sense, to date there is little specific research that we can draw on to help inform how to go about it.[29] However, based on 'best evidence' we suggest four key opportunities which can support a scenario-based, agile talent approach to future needs:

- *Understand and focus on the core future skills.* Access to these skills can become the goal, without necessarily knowing the job roles that these skills will be deployed in. According to research by Deloitte, these future skills are likely to be different from current skills, but there is a lack of understanding about what they will be.[30] However, research by the World Economic Forum[31] has identified complex problem solving, critical thinking and creativity as the top-three skills required for employment success in the future. They have also identified important personal characteristics such as curiosity, initiative, persistence, adaptability, leadership and social/cultural awareness. This is consistent with the approach of organisations such as Google, who describe a commitment to recruiting 'learning animals' rather than people with existing specialist skills.[32] Other research has shown the importance of leaders building connections and relationships to enable them to balance the potentially contradictory demands on them (such as short- and long-term innovation and standardisation) in what has been described as the 'adaptive space'.[33]

- *Secure access to diverse talent pools.* Increasing diversity increases the chance that the organisation has some of the skills and experiences that are needed, including people with 'disruptive' talent who may be required for fundamentally different thinking. The untapped potential of people from diverse backgrounds has already been explored in the first premise of talent liberation, that 'talent is not as scarce as we think'. There is also increasing interest in looking at the 'talent ecosystem' to explore ways to access people with diverse talent without needing to employ them. According to Mercer,[34] this changes the focus from owning and managing talent to reaching across organisations to share, develop and collaborate with people who have the skills and experiences which the organisation wants to access.

- *Develop speedy feedback loops.* It is essential for the organisation to quickly recognise and respond to emerging talent needs. This is likely to be developed based on understanding the risks. Thus, in some areas of the business, it may be possible to have a fairly stable plan with emerging needs reviewed on an annual (or other) basis. For other businesses (or parts of the business), it may be appropriate to review emerging needs more regularly, for example, in a rapidly emerging marketplace, when integrating newly acquired businesses or when a number of very different strategy scenarios are being considered.

- *Ensure responsive recruitment, training and development capability.* This capability needs to enable immediate gaps to be quickly filled. This can be done either by engaging people within the organisation or by looking at the wider talent ecosystem. Whichever approach is taken, access to quality data is essential. This includes data on someone's skills, motivations, experiences and availability so that a match can be made. There are a number of systems that are designed to help with this. For example, the Australian-based

Adepto[35] can help with identifying available external talent. It also provides the opportunity to look at future availability. This can inform the longer-term actions to fill the potential gaps and thus lead into recruitment, engagement, retention and learning and development planning to secure 'ready now' talent when it will be needed.

Responding to strategic change is core to talent liberation. The ways in which this can be practically applied will be further explored in the following chapters.

Formal processes are only part of the answer

$3 trillion cost. According to a research paper published by Gary Hamel and Michele Zanini, that is the cost of bureaucracy in the United States.[36] Working through the Management Innovation Exchange (MIX),[37] they are now on a quest to help organisations to break free from bureaucracy, to release greater productivity and to be more innovative, flexible and adaptable. But this requires a huge mindset shift from using process and policy to drive compliance and competence to a series of approaches which encourage people to use their initiative, creativity and passion and to go beyond the job description and KPIs.

We suggest that if we want to liberate the talent in our organisation, we need to focus on the outcomes we want to achieve and then take a challenging look at the processes to see if they are helping or not. We suspect that many formal processes contribute little to achieving the aims of the organisation. Meanwhile, feedback from individuals indicates that formal processes bring little benefit in supporting career development.[38]

There are many published examples of organisations which are focusing on cultural practices rather than formal processes. Most notable are perhaps the case studies cited by Robert Kegan and Lisa Lahey[39] with their focus on creating the conditions for people to learn quickly and to support the learning of their peers. In these organisations, everyone is involved in people development. It's a daily activity that is integrated into the way business is performed rather than a separate set of activities or processes that only occur in response to a reminder email from HR. A talent liberation approach does not imply zero processes; rather it is about being clear what you are trying to achieve and using a range of formal and informal approaches to support this, recognising that formal processes can have some unintended consequences.

Taking a talent liberation approach to formal processes, we suggest that there are four key questions to consider when considering formal talent processes:

- *What is the purpose of this process?* How will this process improve your organisation in the short or long term, and is it worth the investment of time? It could be that one process brilliantly implemented will have greater impact than lots of processes which are largely held within HR rather than bringing benefits within the business. For example, Marc Effron, founder and president of the Talent Strategy Group, recommends fundamentally simplifying talent processes, eliminating complexity and only including the parts that add real value.[40]

- *How does this process fit with the culture of the organisation?* As indicated in Chapter 1, fitting processes to the prevailing culture is important.[41] For example, a review of talent by the executive team is only likely to be objective and constructive if there are open, trusting relationships among those taking part. However, if (as we have observed) there is game-playing and competitiveness among members of the executive team, there will be different agendas. Hence some directors might be keen to suggest that they have the best people and to try to discredit the talent of their peers. Alternatively they may want to keep quiet about their talent, for fear of 'poaching' or 'headhunting'.

- *What informal or cultural practices could support these aims?* The purpose you are trying to achieve might best be achieved through a combination of formal and informal approaches. In this context, the informal may include any activity that is not formally managed and tracked. For example, if the aim is to help everyone to move closer to their Personal Best, then there is a role for informal career conversations, supported through providing education, training and encouragement, but not necessarily a formal process. Similarly, informal conversations could be used to support people with High Potential to navigate their career options. Our research suggests that people find huge value in such ad-hoc conversations, leading to higher engagement, performance and development.

- *What might be some unintended consequences of this process?* Many formal processes and rules bring unintended consequences,[42] and the same happens within talent. For example, people identified as 'High Potential' report feeling pressure and anxiety about their ability to perform, which can negatively impact their performance. They may also have higher expectations of how the organisation will support them, leaving them feeling dissatisfied with the level of support and guidance that they actually receive.[43]

Consideration of informal processes, culture and values is consistent with case study research on successful organisations. For example, Jeffery Pfeffer, in his book *Hidden Value*,[44] concluded that competitive advantage lay not in exceptional individual leadership talent but in the values, alignment of people-centred practices and the CEOs focus on the values. It seems that to focus on securing individuals with specific skills but not to create an environment where these skills can be used for ongoing benefit is surely to miss the point of a talent strategy. We therefore believe that a balance of formal and informal processes is fundamental to an effective talent strategy. Further examples and practical tools are given in the following chapters.

Success depends on partnership between the organisation and the people

Customer excellence continues to be a key goal for many organisations. KPMG research with 54,000 consumers across 14 markets has identified that organisations recognised for their customer excellence invest in building deep understanding of their customers.[45] Their insights get under the skin of what their customers want and need, and the organisation consistently delivers. These organisations are responsive and able to personalise. They also align their customer experience with their employee experience, ensuring their workforce is engaged and empowered with a compelling sense of purpose.

It's not new to think of your employees as your customers or to see the leadership role as serving their needs.[46] However, a review of employee engagement suggests that it remains rare.[47] In order to see employees as customers, the focus needs to be on the employment relationship as a partnership, a relationship where both parties' needs can be met and where individuals can thrive. As we saw in Chapter 2, the landscape of careers appears to be changing. To liberate talent requires us to dig a little deeper, to understand what people want from work and to find ways to meet their needs alongside the needs of the organisation. This requires us to find ways that fit with all the talent quadrants: to find ways of helping people to achieve their Personal Best; to understand and use people's Strengths; to identify and develop people with High Potential and, where appropriate, to work with people who are Gifted. In some instances, this may signal a long-term relationship based on mutual expectations, loyalty and investment. In other situations, this may be more transactional, with the career deal comprising set pay for set work with little expectation of a broader or more fulfilling contribution.

A number of features of partnership emerge in the talent research, which can be applied to talent liberation.

- *Clear career deal.* The value of a transparent relationship with a clear 'deal' is important. From the organisation's point of view, this will be partly made up of your employee value proposition, but this then needs to be personalised to match the aspirations and needs of the role and the individual. It has been suggested[48] that where possible, workers and their manager engage in explicit 'career contracting' to ensure mutual understanding of what is wanted and what is offered. This clearly links with the customer model of building understanding of customer needs to ensure these can be met, with ongoing reviews from both parties.
- *Shared accountability for career development.* Accountability for career development can be shared such that both the employee and the organisation

recognise their role and have the skills and resources to enact this. There is much talk of employees 'owning their own career', but few organisations actively engage in helping their workers to build career management skills.[49]

- *Meaningful work.* Research has found that work which gave the opportunity for people to develop towards their desired future career (or 'future work self') was considered particularly meaningful.[50] In particular, the findings suggest that roles which give people the opportunity to use different skills, to have flexibility in how and when they work and where they get regular feedback are likely to be experienced as meaningful. The sense of meaningfulness is likely to increase when the work is aligned with personal aspirations.

- *Line manager as 'broker'.* The line manager emerges as an important 'broker' in helping to find the overlap between what the organisation needs and what the individual wants.[51] This makes sense because the line manager is closest to both stakeholders and should be the one engaging in regular dialogue with the person about their current performance, motivation and future hopes. Furthermore, managers directly influence the way people experience the culture, the level of engagement and motivation, all important elements of a successful career and talent partnership.

These elements of talent liberations are explored further in Chapter 6 (leader as liberator) and Chapter 7 (liberating your own talent).

Reflections

We offer talent liberation as an alternative way of thinking about the talent challenges being faced by organisations. We suggest that these premises for the talent agenda will help organisations to find talent approaches that are suited to the changes in macrostructures, internal structures, demographics, technology and career that were explored in the previous chapter. It calls to mind a story told by Cilian Fennell, Irish broadcaster and communications expert.[52] Talking about the Ten Commandments in the Bible, he says it's easier to follow them if, instead of focusing on 'thou shalt not . . .', you think 'you're better off if you don't . . .'. It is in that spirit that we offer these principles. Based on the evidence we have seen, when it comes to talent, we think that 'you're better off if you see that talent is not as scarce as you think; that high performance is a result of teams as well as individuals; that we need to be responsive to changing talent needs; that formal processes are only part of the answer and that success depends on partnership between the organisation and the people'. As indicated previously, other writers, academics and practitioners have previously drawn attention to some of these ideas. However, bringing these premises together provides a new and coherent framework for improving our response to the current talent challenges we face. In writing this book, we have reflected on why it hasn't been done before. We concluded that in part the 'illusory truth effect' may be in operation. The language of the 'war for talent', 'talent scarcity' and tools such as nine-box grid have been so often repeated that they are taken as truth.[53] The fixation with short-term results and the difficulty of looking at cultural contributions to talent also makes it more attractive to focus on the easier-to-control approaches of people and practices.

To help you to reflect on what you have read, we now pose some talent liberation questions. We hope these can help you to consider your current frame of reference for thinking about talent, uncovering assumptions you may hold and how they influence your approach. The questions here are focused on raising your awareness. In the following chapters, we move on to explore a clearer picture of what is going on and then to develop solutions.

It can help to discuss it with some other people. We have referred to 'your organisation', and this could be your whole organisation if you have a senior leadership or cross-business role. Equally, this could refer to your part of the organisation as the principles could apply just as much to a smaller team.

Talent is not as scarce as we think:

- How difficult is it for you to find the talented people you want and need?
- How does your view on scarcity influence your mindset and your actions?
- How is 'talent scarcity' discussed by other people in your organisation?
- What is the impact of this?

High Performance is a result of teams and individuals:

- How does your organisation recognise and support high performance in individuals?
- What is the contribution of high-performing teams, and how is this recognised?
- How do you set teams up for success?
- What is the impact of this?

We need to be responsive to changing talent needs:

- How future focused is your approach to talent?
- How conscious are you of the need for agility and flexibility in your talent strategy?
- How much focus is there on the benefits of diversity?
- How responsive is your talent approach?
- What is the impact of this?

Formal processes are only part of the answer:

- What outcomes are you trying to achieve through your talent strategy?
- How well does the culture support or undermine these aims?
- How much attention do you give to the role of informal practices?
- What is the impact of this?

Success depends on partnership between the organisation and the people:

- How much support is there for a partnership approach?
- What do line managers see as their role in supporting career development?
- How transparent are you about the career deal and career opportunities?
- What is the impact of this?

Notes

1 For an example of using metaphor to explore new paradigms and driving change, see Norris, S. E., 2017. Examining the strategic leadership of organizations using metaphor: Brains and flux-interconnected and interlocked. In: *Encyclopedia of strategic leadership and management*. Hershey, PA: IGI Global, 1337–1353.
2 See Ralph Stacey's book, 2010. *Strategic management and organisational dynamics: The challenge of complexity*, 6th ed, Pearson, for a comprehensive discussion on these issues.
3 E.g. See UhlBien, M. and Marion, R. eds., 2007. *Complexity leadership: Part 1: Conceptual foundations*. Charlotte, NC: IAP.
4 For further information on the manifesto, visit http://agilemanifesto.org/ (accessed 29.06.2019).
5 There are lots of articles on the use of agile and the benefits of this to IT and other functions. For evidence of the positive impact of agile, see Serrador, P. and Pinto, J. K., 2015. Does Agile work? – A quantitative analysis of agile project success. *International Journal of Project Management* 33(5), 1040–1051. For information on the wider adoption of agile, see McKinsey 2017 showing that adopting agile approaches is a key strategic priority for many organisations, particularly those operating in more volatile environment where there are greater perceived rewards, www.mckinsey.com/business-functions/organization/our-insights/how-to-create-an-agile-organization (accessed 08.07.2019).
6 The application of agile in HR is explored in a 2017 article by Jeff Gothelf in HBR (https://hbr.org/2017/06/how-hr-can-become-agile-and-why-it-needs-to (all accessed 30.04.2019).
For more information on the agile HR manifesto and the signatures, visit www.agileh rmanifesto.org/
7 This helpful article summarises some of the agile HR approaches, based on a review in HBR www.forbes.com/sites/stevedenning/2018/03/11/can-hr-become-agile/# 783c86164ae3 (accessed 17.06.2019).
8 © 2001, the Agile Manifesto authors 'This declaration may be freely copied in any form, but only in its entirety through this notice'. This and the five principles can be found at the website, www.agilehrmanifesto.org/ (accessed 18.06.2019).

9 The British Medical Council has an online tool that enables you to search for data on numbers of registrations in different categories from 2006 to present, https://data.gmc-uk.org/gmcdata/home/#/reports/The%20Register/Stats/report (accessed 17.06.2019).

10 http://www3.weforum.org/docs/GGGR16/WEF_Global_Gender_Gap_Report_2016.pdf (accessed 17.06.2019).

11 For the full report, see the 2017 report from the Institute for Policy Studies, https://prosperitynow.org/files/PDFs/road_to_zero_wealth.pdf (accessed 18.06.2019).

12 For a summary of day one of the conference, visit www.salzburgglobal.org/news/latest-news/article/untapped-talent-day-1-can-better-testing-and-data-accelerate-creativity-yes-it-can.html (accessed 18.06.2019).

13 Cross, R., Cowen, A., Vertucci, L. and Thomas, R. J., 2009. Leading in a connected world: How effective leaders drive results through networks. *Organizational dynamics* 38(2), 93–105.

14 The reasons for this lack of visibility can be numerous. For example, under-represented groups may not have the same 'social capital' to enable them to build the relationships, demonstrate their capability and speak up. This in turn can lead to them being given less challenging assignment and fewer opportunities to develop and grow, which exacerbates the problem. For a summary of these issues from a diversity perspective, see Frost, S. and Kalman, D., 2016. *Inclusive talent management: How business can thrive in an age of diversity.* London: Kogan Page.

15 For examples, see Bibb, S., 2016. *Strengths-based recruitment and development: A practical guide to transforming talent management strategy for business results.* London: Kogan Page Publishers.

16 Dweck, C., 2012. *Mindset: Changing the way you think to fulfil your potential.* New York: Hachette UK.

17 See www.bbc.co.uk/sport/football/36166146 for an analysis of the cost of the squad that year for the whole League (accessed 18.06.2019).

18 www.theguardian.com/football/blog/2016/may/02/leicester-city-champions-premier-league (accessed 18.06.2019).

19 For further evidence and a review of the literature, it is helpful to read Alison Mackey's article, Mackey, A., 2008. The effect of CEOs on firm performance. *Strategic Management Journal* 29(12), 1357–1367.

20 Pfeffer, J., 2001. Fighting the war for talent is hazardous to your organization's health. *Organizational Dynamics* 29(4), 248–259.

21 For example, David Collings describes research from film and sports that suggest that the additional cost of the 'stars' cancels out the additional revenue. Collings, D. G., 2014. Toward mature talent management: Beyond shareholder value. *Human Resource Development Quarterly* 25(3), 301–319.

22 For an example of this, see Barney, J. B., 2001. Resource-based theories of competitive advantage: A ten-year retrospective on the resource-based view. *Journal of Management* 27(6), 643–650. For an article relating the Resource Based View to talent management, see Bowman, C. and Hird, M., 2014. A resource based view of talent management. In: P. Sparrow, H. Scullion and I. Tarique, eds., *Strategic talent management: Contemporary issues in international context.* Cambridge: Cambridge University Press.

23 For example, see the original work on the AMO approach to performance: Appelbaum, E., Bailey, T., Berg, P. B., Kalleberg, A. L. and Bailey, T. A., 2000. *Manufacturing advantage: Why high-performance work systems pay off.* Ithaca, NY: Cornell University Press. There has also be considerable follow-up research by authors such as Boxall, Guest, and Boselie.

24 For example, see the Bath Model of people and performance, Purcell, J., 2003. *Understanding the people and performance link: Unlocking the black box.* London: CIPD Publishing.

25 Maynard, M. T., Vartiainen, M. and Sanchez, D., 2017. Virtual teams: Utilizing talent management thinking to assess what we currently know about making virtual teams successful. In: D. Collings, K. Mellahi and W. Cascio, eds., *The Oxford handbook of talent management.* Oxford: Oxford University Press, pp. 193–214.

26 This is cited as one of the main challenges for strategic HR Management. See Lepak, D. P., Jiang, K. and Ployhart, R., 2017. HR strategy, structure, and architecture. In: P. Sparrow and C. Cooper, eds., *A research agenda for human resource management*, Cheltenham, UK: Edwards Elgar Publishing, pp. 23–38. The mutual influence and interplay between high potential employees (or 'stars') and teams is explored in Kehoe, R. R., Rosikiewicz, B. L. and Tzabbar, D., 2017. Talent and teams. In: *Oxford handbook of talent management*, pp. 153–168.

27 See www.forbes.com/sites/karstenstrauss/2017/02/08/the-toughest-jobs-to-fill-in-2017/#e5761ee7f143 for the complete list (accessed 18.06.2019).

28 See Cascio, W. F., Boudreau, J. W. and Church, A. H., 2017. Using a risk-optimisation lens: Maximising talent readiness for an uncertain future. In: *A research agenda for human resource management*. Cheltenham, UK: Edward Elgar Publishing, pp. 55–77.

29 Some talent approaches are challenged for being based on very little solid evidence or peer-reviewed academic literature. However, in the absence of such evidence, we are using the 'best available' evidence, as suggested by the Center for Evidence Based Management www.cebma.org/ (accessed 18.02.2019).

30 https://www2.deloitte.com/content/dam/insights/us/articles/GLOB1948_Success-personified-4th-ind-rev/DI_Success-personified-fourth-industrial-revolution.pdf (accessed 18.06.2019).

31 www.weforum.org/agenda/2016/03/21st-century-skills-future-jobs-students/.

32 See https://hbr.org/2014/09/how-google-manages-talent (accessed 06.05.2019).

33 Arena, M. J. and Uhl-Bien, M., 2016. Complexity leadership theory: Shifting from human capital to social capital. *People and Strategy* 39(2), 22.

34 www.mercer.com/our-thinking/building-a-talent-ecosystem.html (accessed 18.06.2019).

35 Founded by Chris Milligan, more information can be found at www.adepto.com/ (accessed 18.06.2019).

36 For details of the research paper, see www.managementexchange.com/sites/default/files/three-trillion-dollars.pdf (accessed 18.06.2019).

37 This is a fascinating platform to encourage sharing of ideas and collaboration www.managementexchange.com/about-the-mix (accessed 18.06.2019).

38 Evans, M. J., 2017. *Workplace career conversations: Aligning organizational talent management and individual career development?* (Doctoral dissertation, © Maggi Evans).

39 Kegan, R. and Lahey, L., 2016. *An everyone culture: Becoming a deliberately developmental organization*. Boston: Harvard Business School Publishing.

40 Effron, M. and Ort, M., 2010. *One page talent management: Eliminating complexity, adding value*. Boston: Harvard Business Press.

41 Garrow, V. and Hirsh, W., 2008. Talent management: Issues of focus and fit. *Public Personnel Management* 37(4), 389–402.

42 For example, the so-called 'cobra effect', where people in India were rewarded for killing cobra in an attempt to reduce the population of the deadly snake. As a result, cobra farms were set up to fulfil the demand for cobra that people could kill so they could earn the reward.

43 Campbell, M. and Smith, R., 2010. *High-potential talent: A view from inside the leadership pipeline*. Greensboro, NC: Center for Creative Leadership. See also Daubner-Siva, D., Ybema, S., Vinkenburg, C. J. and Beech, N., 2018. The talent paradox: Talent management as a mixed blessing. *Journal of Organizational Ethnography* 7(1), 74–86.

44 O'Reilly III, C. A. and Pfeffer, J., 2000. *Hidden value: How great companies achieve extraordinary results with ordinary people*. Boston: Harvard Business School Press.

45 To download a copy of the report, you can register at https://marketing.kpmg.co.uk/global-customer-cee-report/ (accessed 18.06.2019).

46 The concept of 'servant leadership' is popular in leadership development and academic research. See Greenleaf, R. K., 2002. *Servant leadership: A journey into the nature of legitimate power and greatness*. New York: Paulist Press. For more background.

47 Pfeffer, J., 2015. *Leadership BS: Fixing workplaces and careers one truth at a time.* New York: Harper Collins.

48 See Herriot, P. and Pemberton, C., 1995. *New deals: The revolution in managerial careers.* Chichester: John Wiley & Son Ltd.

49 Our research indicated that whilst most HR professionals see the individual as responsible for managing their own career, little support is given, https://dspace.lboro.ac.uk/dspace-jspui/bitstream/2134/27036/3/Thesis-2017-Evans.pdf (accessed 09.05.2019).

50 For more information, see Boeck, G., Dries, N. and Tierens, H., 2019. The experience of untapped potential: Towards a subjective temporal understanding of work meaningfulness. *Journal of Management Studies* 56(3), 529–557.

51 For example, see Hirsh, W., 2008. *Career development in employing organisations: Practices and challenges from a UK perspective.* London: Institute for Employment Studies. This shows the importance of line managers' involvement in career development.

52 Cilian is Director of Stillwater Communications, http://stillwater.ie/ (accessed 18.06.2019).

53 For a summary of this effect, see https://digest.bps.org.uk/2019/06/26/higher-intelligence-and-an-analytical-thinking-style-offer-no-protection-against-the-illusory-truth-effect-our-tendency-to-believe-repeated-claims-are-more-likely-to-be-true/ (accessed 29.06.2019).

Part II

The practice of talent liberation

4 The Talent Compass – identifying risks and opportunities

Introduction

In the last chapter we identified the five premises underpinning the talent liberation approach: talent is not as scarce as we think; high performance is a result of teams as well as individuals; we need to be responsive to changing talent needs; formal processes are only part of the answer and success depends on partnership between the organisation and the people. In particular, we showed how applying these premises could help to drive competitive advantage through increased performance. We now want to make things more practical, to move from the metaphor of talent liberation to start exploring how you can use this approach to help you in your organisation. To do this, we're going to introduce a tool to help you to capture the different parts of the system so you can see how they interact. We have called this tool the Talent Compass, as it will help you to navigate your way around the talent system in your organisation. Having introduced the tool, we will look at each element in turn, explaining what it covers and why it matters and suggesting some questions to help you to develop insights relevant to your organisation. These questions will help you to build on and refine your answers to the coaching questions at the end of the previous chapter. We finish the chapter with some examples of how the Talent Compass helps you to build a holistic view of your strengths and risks in relation to your talent strategy. These insights can then be used to develop plans for action. More details on applying the Talent Compass and talent liberation to different stakeholder groups (HR, leaders and individuals) are then given in the following chapters.

Overview of the Talent Compass

We have positioned talent liberation as taking place within a system. We have already referenced different stakeholders and influences within this system such as the cultural climate within the organisation and some of the broader ways that the world of work seems to be changing. So how does it all fit together? What are the key pieces of the system, and how do they interconnect? As suggested by systems thinkers, representing the system is a helpful first step in understanding it and thinking about how to influence change. Our early attempts at mapping the system with clients were a bit piecemeal, depending on the issue we were focusing on. This reinforced to us that each organisation is different and there is no single map that will work for all organisations. So we set ourselves a challenge: how could we take the complexity of a constantly evolving system and represent it in a practical way? How could we develop a way to represent the five talent liberation premises and to reflect the changing world of work? How could we move beyond the typical diagrams which illustrate employee life cycle or workforce planning? How could we represent the system at an organisational, business unit, functional or team level in one diagram?

We drew inspiration from others who have tackled similar challenges. In particular, we found the approach of the Business Model Canvas[1] helpful in the way it illustrated the possibility of presenting different elements of a strategy on one page and using this as a framework for conversations about possibilities, challenges and innovations at different levels in an organisation. The principles in Lafley and Martin's book, *Playing to Win: how strategy really works,*[2] were also helpful. Particularly that strategy is about making choices, there is no single perfect strategy and good strategy combines creativity and rigour.

It is in this context that we offer our Talent Compass (see Figure 4.1), helping you to navigate through the talent landscape in your organisation. As with any representation, it is not perfect, and it involves simplification. However, using

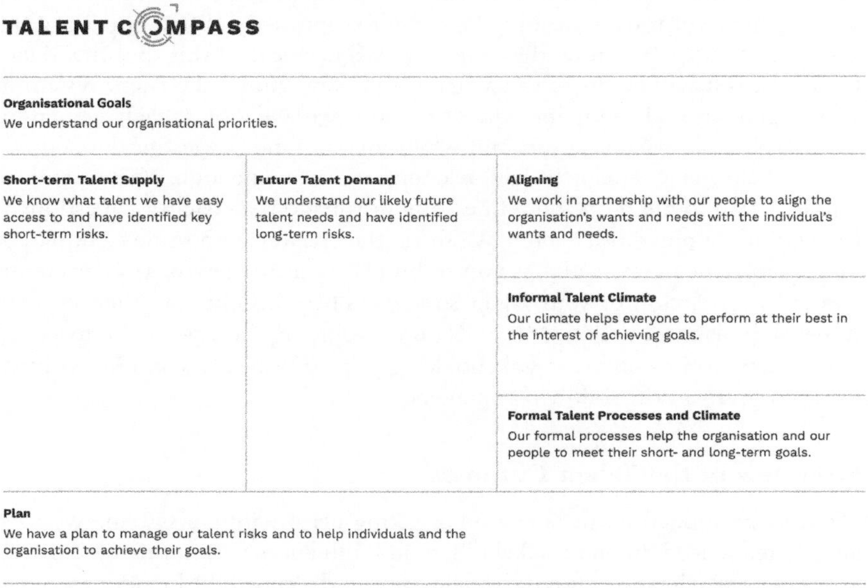

TALENT COMPASS

Organisational Goals
We understand our organisational priorities.

Short-term Talent Supply	**Future Talent Demand**	**Aligning**
We know what talent we have easy access to and have identified key short-term risks.	We understand our likely future talent needs and have identified long-term risks.	We work in partnership with our people to align the organisation's wants and needs with the individual's wants and needs.
		Informal Talent Climate Our climate helps everyone to perform at their best in the interest of achieving goals.
		Formal Talent Processes and Climate Our formal processes help the organisation and our people to meet their short- and long-term goals.

Plan
We have a plan to manage our talent risks and to help individuals and the organisation to achieve their goals.

Figure 4.1 The Talent Compass

Registered design number: 6063526

it with clients we have found it to provide a powerful lens through which to conceptualise and differentiate parts of a talent strategy. Capturing this on one page helps to represent the complexity of the talent agenda in an accessible way without oversimplifying.

We start with an assumption that you already have a sense of your strategic aims and that you see the opportunity to improve your approach to talent in order to increase your competitive advantage (or to improve your service delivery if in a not-for-profit organisation). Although we see the Talent Compass as representing a system, we have not drawn in arrows. Our assumption is that each part of the diagram is likely to influence and be influenced by other parts. Likewise, each part is not discrete, and sometimes it is difficult to decide where to put things. For example, does assessment fit best under short-term talent supply or as a formal talent process? Our primary goal is to capture a range of connected points to discuss and consider, to build a comprehensive picture of talent in your organisation to help you to develop appropriate plans. It is also our expectation that by going through the Talent Compass, you will identify new actions and priorities that you had not considered when working through the more familiar talent management processes which could limit you to the typical talent management strategies of planning, attraction, development or retention.[3] In particular, the insights can help you to frame and address the priority issues, those that will help you to minimise and mitigate risks and to take advantage of opportunities.

As we have refined and developed the Talent Compass, we have evolved a number of questions that we use when discussing it with clients. We see these questions as points to consider and as conversation starters – not the entire agenda. We recognise that going through the questions can be a little overwhelming, so it can be helpful to choose which you feel are the most important questions for you to consider. It is also important to notice the things that you are doing well rather than just to focus on the gaps in your current approach. A summary of the questions is provided within each section later, with more detailed questions given in Chapter 8. You may also choose to go through the Talent Compass with different stakeholder groups. For example, it can stimulate important board-level conversations as well as develop new understanding at a business-unit level and with the HR team.

The Talent Compass has been developed as a very practical tool that can help you to consider the whole talent landscape in your organisation and use these insights to identify specific actions that you can take to liberate talent and gain greater competitive advantage. Some of these actions will be specifically related to a particular talent quadrant (such as understanding more about an individual's Strengths). Other actions will apply to more than one quadrant (such as supporting individual development with the goal of helping everyone to achieve their Personal Best and providing targeted development for those seen as High Potential). Similarly, these actions may relate to formal aspects of talent management (such as refining succession planning or assessment of learning agility), or they may be more cultural, finding ways to set teams up for success. Alternatively, the actions you take may involve technology solutions so you have greater visibility of the talent you have and the talent you can access through your external networks, or you may focus your attention on helping individuals to lead and manage their own career. There is no single 'right' solution.

Organisational goals

We understand our organisational priorities

Meeting organisational goals has always been positioned as the fundamental driver for any work on talent. Whatever description of talent is being used and whatever the approach, a key input to the action plan and rationale has to be the organisational goals. However, as discussed in the previous chapters, it should be recognised that the goals are fluid and will change. The overall purpose and direction of the organisation may remain relatively constant, but market changes, technological innovations and economic cycles will all impact on the goals and the plans for how they are best achieved.

Given the third premise of talent liberation to be responsive to changing talent needs, we need to capture the possible scenarios that the talent strategy should be prepared for. These scenarios may never materialise. However, as Shell has found since spearheading the use of scenarios in the 1970s, there are huge benefits in exploring possibilities and learning from them.[4]

Each scenario will drive different aims and approaches for talent in terms of skills and experiences of people you need and the behaviours that you value and reward. In addition to these differences, there are likely to be some similarities in aims. For example, with people being the biggest cost base for many organisations, one common goal tends to be the importance of an engaged and productive workforce. We are also finding that whichever core strategy organisations are adopting, there is a focus on building greater collaboration and agility into their structure. Similarly, we tend to agree with Tomas Chamorro-Premuzic in that it is increasingly important for people to demonstrate self-awareness, curiosity and entrepreneurship[5] to enable them to thrive in the current work environment.

Key questions:

- What are your key strategic aims?
- What do you see as your organisational strengths, weaknesses, opportunities and threats?
- What values shape the way your organisation operates?
- What are the possible scenarios for how your organisation may evolve and grow (e.g. new markets, products, services, or technology)?
- What are the organisational priorities and risks that the talent strategy needs to address?

This digital service provider employs 70,000 people worldwide. They operate in a highly volatile market and need to respond rapidly to their clients' needs, doing it better than anyone else could. This places agility at the centre of their strategy. They don't know the nature of the change, but they know that in any year, they will be scaling up in some areas, downsizing others and developing new services, whilst retaining their reputation for service excellence. They need to address a number of risks: the supply of leaders who can quickly adapt and lead their part of the organisation through change; team members who are open to learning new skills and relationships with third parties to help them to quickly scale up as a new business opportunity emerges. This captures their three biggest talent priorities within the context of their goals.

Short-term talent supply

We know what talent we have easy access to and
have identified key short-term risks

Understanding the current talent supply is an obvious step in developing your talent plan, capturing the skills, knowledge and experience that your organisation has easy access to. These may be the people employed by you, but equally it may include some easy-to-secure contractors or outsourced support across your talent ecosystem (a topic further explored in the next chapter). With many other business resources such as stock, it's relatively easy to conduct an audit of what you have or what you can readily acquire, looking through inventories and discussing with partners to calculate a fairly accurate picture. However, when it comes to current talent supply, it is not as easy to develop a reliable answer, and key people may choose to leave you with little warning. The data you can produce will inevitably involve compromise and judgement. It will not be perfect, but to create perfect data would be an industry in itself and not necessarily in the interests of achieving the organisation's aims.

In order to collect information on short-term talent supply, there will need to be some prioritisation of which roles are most important. It has been suggested that roles can be categorised by strategic importance.[6] So, for example, many large banks and retailers recognise that branch managers play a critical role in delivering results. Moreover, research suggests that people tend to be successful in roles if appointed internally rather than as an external recruit.[7] Consequently, it is appropriate to invest time in understanding the current talent in these roles and the short-term potential for people to move into these roles. Similarly, for utility companies, the current supply of engineers with specific skills sets is an essential piece of organisational data. These groups would therefore be in strategically critical roles. There is also a case for collecting some data on other roles/populations. For example, as discussed earlier, with people being the largest cost, there is a desire for everyone to be performing well. Thus, collecting data to estimate the extent to which everyone is performing at (or close to) their Personal Best becomes valuable.

The approach to measurement will depend on how important it is for you to have accurate data. Thus, there is likely to be more investment in collecting data for the strategically important roles than for others. Generally, it is better to rely on a number of sources of data rather than just one as this increases confidence in data accuracy.[8] So, whilst recognising that performance ratings have many problems, their usefulness can be increased if they are combined with additional data such as customer ratings, 360 feedback, financial results, team engagement and surveys. Organisations with access to comprehensive Human Capital Management systems (such as Workday or PeopleSoft) will find it easier to access and use broader range of data than other organisations.

Questions:

- Which are the strategically most important skills, knowledge, experience and roles in the short term?
- What is your visibility of your current supply of people with these skills in these roles?
- What difficulties have you encountered in the past 12 months in finding people with the skills, experience and knowledge that you need?
- What changes do you anticipate to this supply in the short term?
- What are the risks that emerge from reviewing these questions?

This technology organisation has just won a large, high-profile contract. To successfully deliver this, they need to rapidly increase the number of developers they have working in this part of the business. They suspect that there is some spare resource in other parts of the organisation that could be redeployed. However, there is little visibility of who might be available and what skills they have. They have had initial conversations with recruitment agencies, and it seems that there is a general lack of people available with the skills they are looking for. This highlights a delivery risk and a need to better understand the availability of people internally who could fulfil the roles and to explore alternative sources of supply.

Future talent demand

We understand our likely future talent needs and have identified long-term risks

What might be the future talent requirements of the business in order to meet the organisational goals and different scenarios? Historically organisations were often able to develop detailed forecasts based on robust assumptions regarding the nature of work, the number of retirees and business growth. It was these data that gave large manufacturing companies the confidence to recruit set numbers of apprenticeships each year. However, as we have established, identifying future needs in the current climate is a best estimate rather than an exact science. Therefore, in establishing future demand, we need to not only identify gaps but also look for ways to build in contingency and to mitigate the risk of our estimates being wrong.[9] As indicated in the previous chapters, this risk management lens emphasises the importance of building agility into the talent approach, ensuring access to diverse talent pools, disruptive talent and a focus on the 'human skills'. It also highlights the value of considering a combination of internal and external options for how to source people with the required talent rather than a reactive reliance on external sourcing of people with 'ready now' talent. One of the other themes that emerges is the sometimes unforeseen cost of external recruits. In many roles it takes a long time for people to become fully productive in new roles, and as we saw in Chapter 2, there is a high failure rate for external recruits.[10]

When thinking about future demands, it's important to be realistic. Richard Eardley is managing director for Hays in Asia. His team frequently get requests for recruits who 'must have at least five years' experience in technology x'. However, this technology has only been around for five years. The people with five years of experience are the gurus. They are more expensive and more skilled than the client needs, and they wouldn't be interested in the role. This underlines the importance of shifting thinking from the 'ready now' skills to look for people who show an appropriate way of thinking, who have some relevant skills and who are motivated to learn. These people are often the best fit, but it requires realism and a bit of forward planning. If you wait until it's urgent, then it's too late. Similarly, it is worth reflecting on how you measure someone's competence. In a world of easy access to quality learning, people may be self-taught in a skill or discipline without having a formal qualification. Consequently, setting essential criteria for new recruits of particular qualifications may be unnecessarily limiting the pool of people whom you consider suitable with knock-on effects on diversity and may require alternative assessment methods.

A further element of future talent demand is the role of high-performing teams in addition to high-performing individuals. Considering the role and contribution of teams to your future success will help to shape the skills and experience that are needed.

Questions:

- What are the key talent implications for each scenario explored as part of your organisational goals?
- What are the key gaps between what you have now and what you need in the future?
- How confident are you that these gaps can be filled (internally or externally)?
- What alternative sources could you explore to fill any of these gaps?
- What are the risks that emerge from reviewing these questions?

This organisation is responsible for providing community-based care for the elderly and other vulnerable people. The organisation is aiming to grow, but has identified that growth may be limited by the lack of availability of people with the appropriate skills, attitude and commitment to be successful care workers. Care work is challenging, and although rewarding, it can be highly pressured and is often not well paid. The organisation is growing, but turnover is high. There is no additional source of internal talent, and many sources of external talent (including overseas recruitment) have also been exhausted. Thus, in the short term, the resource needs can just be met, but there is a clear longer-term risk that could restrict expansion and ongoing service delivery. A new approach to talent needs to be found so that long-term needs can be met.

Aligning

We work in partnership with our people to align the organisation's wants and needs with the individual's wants and needs

Aligning is an essential element of the Talent Compass to bring a focus on our fifth premise, that success depends on a partnership between the organisation and the individual. With the changing nature of work, such an approach seems important. Although aligning provides opportunities for meeting both individual and organisational needs, there has been surprisingly little academic research specifically into this.[11] However, matching incorporates a number of elements of HR management that are often spoken about. For example, as described in Chapter 2, employee experience is gaining popularity as a lens for creating a place where people *want* to work rather than assuming people work largely because they need to.[12] The components of engagement (such as those suggested by Gallop) often incorporate measures related to use of personal strengths, the opportunity to learn and the sense that the individual can grow their career. The work on meaning described in the previous chapter also creates a framework to think about aligning. Other elements of engagement (such as feeling cared about) relate more closely to the informal talent climate (which we will discuss in the next section). Aligning also relates to employer branding, the image that the company projects and the experiences people working there share. This information helps potential recruits (and existing staff) gain a sense of whether this is a place they want to work. Does the image align with their identity and what they want from work?

For many organisations, the challenge of aligning is that it represents a fundamentally different mindset. It involves consciously positioning the individual as a stakeholder in all discussions and decisions regarding their work. This doesn't need to be based on an altruistic desire for individuals to thrive for their own sake. Rather it can be based on a recognition that those who do want to work with you will be more engaged, perform better, adapt better and represent you better compared with those who don't. Evidence being collected by the Maturity Institute[13] is showing how a focus on Total Stakeholder Value (rather than the more limited shareholder value) is generating greater material value and lower risk. This is premised on finding ways to support mutual goals for all stakeholder groups. They reference Toyota and Handelsbanken as examples of this way of operating, showing how a whole system approach can reduce risk and enhance value. In essence, better aligning can create an environment where more people are close to their Personal Best, where High Potential is developed and Personal Strengths are utilised. This enables the whole system to fully leverage skills, knowledge and experiences.

Along with the mindset change is a need for greater transparency. As described in the previous chapter, the best alignment is achieved when there is a clear and regularly reviewed 'deal'. The idea of transparent career contracting was suggested back in the 1990s,[14] but there is little evidence that such transparent career conversations are taking place outside the recruitment process.[15] Moreover, what people want may vary at different stages in their career. For example, for those in later career, hierarchical career advancement opportunities are typically less of an engagement driver than they are for other groups.[16] So aligning is an ongoing process. It applies to everyone in the talent ecosystem, and the more transparent it is, the greater the opportunity to benefit.

Questions:

- How clear are you on the wants and needs of the people you work with?
- In what ways do you create a shared understanding, transparency and matching of wants and needs?
- How attractive is your organisation for existing and potential workers in terms of financial, benefits, developmental opportunities, flexibility and other features?
- What are the risks that emerge from reviewing these questions?

This engineering organisation employs highly skilled and talented engineers on a range of global projects. Many of these engineers value the opportunity to get involved in challenging assignments and to stretch their technical abilities, valuing this more than hierarchical progression. The organisation is able to attract talented external people based on the nature of these assignments. However, once in a role it can be difficult for people to have visibility of other opportunities. Consequently, they can feel that their needs are not being taken into account, resulting in lower motivation and some people choosing to leave. Understanding the needs and aspirations of these people can help to identify ways to match what they want with what the organisation needs.

Informal talent climate

*Our climate helps everyone to perform at their best in the
interests of achieving the organisation's goals*

The informal talent climate captures the way that people experience working in
the organisation. It focuses on the behaviours, the way that policy and process
are enacted and the culture. As described in the fourth premise of talent liberation, these features are all highly influential parts of the talent system. Combined,
they will directly impact on all elements of talent including: how well people
are able to work at their Personal Best; how quickly High Potential people are
developed; how people's Strengths are used, how attractive the organisation is
for people to work with and how well people perform and are retained. There
are many ways of thinking about the informal talent climate, and our thinking
is informed by the work of many others, including Peter Senge (the Learning
organisation), Carol Dweck (growth mindset) and Denise Rousseau (psychological contract). Based on these, we have identified three particular elements to
consider as part of the talent climate: organisation design, organisation culture
and observable behaviours.

Organisation design goes beyond the formal structure chart to include how
work is organised. This includes the extent to which people are empowered,
the way decisions are made, the level of collaboration between parts of the
organisation and the nature of teamwork. The design also covers the opportunity for flexibility in how things are organised, the support for people to
work part time, remotely or in other flexible ways. Culture is a broad topic
and covers 'how things are done round here'. From a talent liberation point of
view, the approach to learning, performance, diversity and risk are particularly
significant parts of culture. A culture that supports talent liberation will have
learning integrated as part of everyday work. The approach to performance
will reinforce a growth mindset where people are constantly developing and
supported to perform at their Personal Best. It will also value learning and
sideways moves as a sign of progression, not just focusing on hierarchical progression. Diversity will be encouraged and supported through role modelling
and an environment that celebrates difference of opinion, background and
beliefs. Importantly, culture also covers the appetite for risk. Many organisations are risk-averse, reluctant to move people early into roles. This has a
negative impact on learning and engagement. Similarly, many are reluctant to
recruit and listen to people with disruptive talent who they may need in order
to evolve and grow their competitive advantage. Observable behaviours within
an organisation are often a result of the design and the culture. This includes
the nature of relationships (such as the extent of mutual respect and trust), the
level of openness and honesty that people display and the behaviours to support performance and growth (such as coaching, feedback, stretch assignments
and clear expectations). In our experience, the informal talent climate is rarely
a part of strategic talent conversations. Therefore in the following chapters, we
will expand these ideas in more detail.

Questions:

- How well do you utilise the skills, knowledge and experiences of your people?
- How well do people work together and collaborate across the organisation?
- How do you encourage and support people to learn and grow?
- What is your appetite for risk in people decisions?
- How open and honest are people in their everyday interactions at work?
- What are the risks that emerge from reviewing these questions?

This global FMCG organisation has a very positive and supportive culture. People use words such as 'love' to describe how they feel about working there. However, there is a less positive implication of this. People avoid having difficult conversations. Consequently, poor performance can go unchallenged, and negative feedback can be so 'dressed up' that people are not clear on how they can or need to improve. It can also lead to people having unrealistic expectations about their potential, finding themselves disappointed when they are not given development opportunities or promotions. Despite these downsides, people continue to stay and be engaged but feel that they are not fulfilling their potential.

Formal talent processes

Our formal processes help the organisation and our people to meet their short- and long-term goals

As described in the previous chapter, we recognise that formal processes have a role to play, but we suggest that on their own they are not enough to drive competitive advantage and may bring some negative unintended consequences. Furthermore processes tend to be developed and implemented for the benefit of the organisation with little or no reference to the individual. This is frequently accompanied by lack of transparency. For example, few organisations share with people that they are part of a High Potential group.[17] We therefore suggest that the contribution of talent processes is reviewed within the overall talent system.

On the whole, we suggest that formal processes should be 'light touch' and based on a very clear purpose or rationale that is aligned with strategic priorities and the informal talent climate. Moreover, we suggest that any processes that are implemented should be evaluated and based on some evidence of what is likely to add value rather than assuming that because others are doing it, it is the right thing to do. To do this, we need greater clarity of evidence to separate out the truly added value from the 'bright and shiny', that promises speed, simplicity and novelty but has no basis in science.[18] This is not to say that we should wait and not action anything until we have seen the evidence. However, it does suggest taking a structured approach, seeking evidence of impact and evaluating the actions we are taking, constantly making improvements and refining our approach based on the evidence we are collecting in a pragmatic way.

Another key point about formal processes is to recognise that they are not a 'drag-and-drop' solution. Research has consistently shown that the processes themselves don't create an impact. Rather it's the way they're done and how they are perceived by the stakeholders. In the case of talent management, these stakeholders are generally being the board, line managers and individuals; however, given the broadening talent ecosystem, this could expand to include people working with the organisation in different ways.[19] Another consequence of this is that any process may need to be adapted for different cultural contexts, so an MNE will need to think carefully about what should be consistent and what should be flexed to meet different cultural contexts.

Established talent processes also benefit from regular reviews to keep them fit for purpose. The following questions should help you to reflect on how these processes are currently working for you. In the next chapter, we explore HR role in adding value through formal process.

Questions:

- What formal talent processes do you use?
- What is the purpose of these, and what value does each add to the organisation and the individual?
- What unintended negative effects do these processes have?
- How do your processes include talented people whom you do not directly employ but make a critical contribution?
- How is individual and team performance recognised and rewarded?
- What career pathways and information is there to help people to map their career?
- What are the risks that emerge from reviewing these questions?

This multinational financial services organisation had a large number of formal processes to help them to manage their talent processes across geographies, business units and technical specialisms. They invested significant amounts of time in developing their senior succession plans, producing an annual succession plan for the top 500 roles. This planning was driven partly by a desire to manage key person risk, but also by a desire to move people between business areas at a senior level to share knowledge and broaden experiences. However, when posts became available, the succession plan was largely ignored, with local 'known' candidates being appointed. This process was therefore not delivering on its purpose. Further research suggested that the data in the succession plan was not trusted. Senior leaders were not confident to take a central recommendation for a position but wanted to select someone who was already known to them.

Plan

We have a plan to manage our talent risks and to help individuals and the organisation to achieve their goals

The plan is the time to review all of the different risks that have been identified in the Talent Compass. As you have gone through it, you are likely to have identified some possible solutions and opportunities for liberating more talent in your organisation. This may, for example, help you to identify an opportunity to deploy people who are Gifted, to more rapidly grow people who have High Potential, to help everyone to perform at their Personal Best and to make use of their Strengths. It may indicate that you need new ways to work across the talent ecosystem in order to access talented people in different ways.

When completing the Talent Compass, it can feel overwhelming, that there is too much to do. To some extent, that's an inevitable consequence of taking a systems approach where everything is seen as interconnected, so it's not simple in the way that a process is. In the plan, we suggest that you keep hold of the complexity but simplify it into a few things that you can influence and act on. Ideally these address the biggest risks and balance the short- and long-term needs of the business. We often find that two or three key themes emerge and the adopted plan combines addressing these themes as well as continuing with existing talent activities. As the plans are developed, it is important to apply good change and project principles. Thus, stakeholders should be involved and engaged, goals should be clarified and budgets agreed as appropriate. Applying the agile approach, it can be helpful to conduct short trials, launching parts of the solution, testing them, learning, refining and then moving to the next part.

The Talent Compass is intended as a dynamic tool. It will always be a work-in-progress rather than a completed plan. When you first use it, you may have lots of questions that you can't answer, lots of missing data. That doesn't matter. You can still use it to inform your action. As you continue to review and develop your Talent Compass, you can add more detail, data, adapt the questions and track how things have changed.

Questions:

- What themes emerge from the whole Talent Compass, and what do you think are the root causes?
- What are you already doing well?
- Which are the biggest short- and long-term talent risks to address?
- How can you leverage aligning informal talent climate and formal processes to address these risks?
- What is the role of HR, line managers and individuals in these solutions?
- How and when will you review the Talent Compass and keep it live?

This Australian-based Fintech organisation has a very positive informal talent climate, and people working there feel supported, stretched, challenged and highly engaged.

The key talent risk they faced was the poor availability of short-term resources. Historically they had engaged with agencies to find people, with 98% of recruits arriving through agencies. This was high cost and inefficient and also gave the organisation little control over the supply. They decided it would be better to approach the market directly rather than through agencies. This enabled them to more actively tell their story, to positively engage with people and to attract people who would fit in and thrive in their organisation. They invested in a graduate intern programme to attract highly talented people so they could experience what it was like to work for this Fintech. They also started actively sharing people's career stories to encourage people to explore alternative career paths and look at a range of internal opportunities. The net effect of this plan was over $1 million savings in recruitment cost, with direct sourcing now at 95%, greater brand recognition from potential recruits and a positive reputation through recognition of a top 10 graduate intern programme.

This public sector organisation provides adult social care services and is experiencing the challenges of a national shortage of experienced, qualified middle managers. Without these managers, it is difficult for them to fulfil their legal obligations in a safe and consistent way. They have identified three primary activities to address this. Firstly, they want to keep their existing people. They therefore focus on creating a positive experience for their current managers and providing growth opportunities for more junior members of the team. They are consciously moving the model of adult social care towards a more positive, strengths-based approach, which staff feel is more aligned with their values and training. Secondly, they are active at promoting this positive work environment to other qualified managers so they can attract them. Thirdly, they are working to increase the supply of suitable middle managers. They are doing this through expanding the talent ecosystem, working in partnership across health to encourage and develop people who have a similar skill set. They are also exploring ways of overcoming some of the potential barriers to people being interested in these roles. To do this, they are testing ways to access their skills in new ways that match the individual and organisational needs, for example, through setting up micro enterprises (businesses set up at very small scale with the intention of generating income rather than building a business).

Company X offers a wide range of business services and employs 70,000 people in more than 40 countries.

Results from their annual engagement survey suggested that people were unsure how to develop their career within the organisation. People knew they were meant to be accountable for their career, but they couldn't see what to do in order to move upwards or across the organisation or to further develop in their current role. This was contributing to retention issues and reducing long-term commitment to the organisation (a problem in short-term talent supply and contributing to long-term talent gaps). Alongside this, the organisation was keen to develop greater agility, so they saw value in people developing their careers across different business units and functions in order to support their strategy. They decided on three key actions. First, they increased the visibility of career pathways, making it clear to people what skills, experiences and knowledge were needed in key roles and illustrating how these could be acquired throughout the organisation. Second, they educated people on how to develop their own career. This encouraged people to build self-awareness, showed how they could broaden their experience and created more open doors so people could talk about their career and aspirations. Third, they trained managers in conducting career conversations so they were able to support team members who wanted career development help. These actions were supported by quarterly education events, which included people sharing their own career stories and a guide with examples, activities and tips. These steps have created far more interest in talking about careers. There are now about 25% more lateral moves, and the most recent engagement survey shows a 15% improvement in response to the question 'my manager talks with me about my career development'.

Reflections

The main tool we have introduced in this chapter is the Talent Compass. It is intended as a dynamic way for you to develop insights about the whole of the talent system that is operating within your organisation. We believe that this approach takes you beyond the typical manpower planning models which are completed just from the organisation's perspective. The Talent Compass also takes you beyond a focus on process and individuals, to include the cultural elements and the enablers of high-performing teams. Finally the approach also incorporates the need for increasing partnership and flexibility and that the talent required may be outside the boundary of the organisation – a network of resources, not just employees.

We suggest that there are different ways to use the Talent Compass. In larger organisations with access to lots of data and resources, you may be able to work through the questions in a structured way to develop a detailed view of how things are and the key risks to address. However, for many organisations, that detailed approach is not possible or appropriate. In these situations, the questions are helpful to increase your understanding of the whole system, and they may indicate some important lines of enquiry. Where you don't have access to comprehensive data, it is still possible to consider what data you do have that could serve as a proxy. (For example, number of accepted offers is a simple indication of employer attractiveness.) You can also collect some data by simply asking people for their views (for example, asking people what they see as the career development role of the organisation, the manager and themselves to understand how clearly the career deal is understood). The other important thing about the compass is that it is just that, a compass, a tool to help you to navigate your way and to guide you. How you use it depends on where you want to get to. It can point you in the right direction, but it can't get you there on its own. A more detailed version of the Talent Compass questions and examples of identified risks and example actions can be found in sections A and B in the Tools and Resources at the end of the book.

Use the following questions to reflect on how you can use the Talent Compass to help you evolve your talent strategy.

- Which bits of the Talent Compass have you previously thought about?
- Which bits are new or different?
- What would you like to understand more about?
- How could the Talent Compass help you to better understand the wider talent system and risks in your organisation?
- Who could help you to have a first go at completing the Talent Compass?
- What are the key risks that you have identified, and what are the wider business implications of these risks?
- What risks have you identified that you already have solutions for?
- And which risks are you unsure about how to address?
- What will you do next?

Notes

1 Business Model Canvas is an approach that helps you to capture business strategy in one page, under nine headings. For a simple introduction, see www.youtube.com/watch?v=QoAOzMTLP5s (accessed 18.06.2019).
2 Lafley, A. G. and Martin, R. L., 2013. *Playing to win: How strategy really works*. Boston: HBR, 2013, is a fascinating way of thinking through strategy, based on the approach taken at Procter & Gamble. It encourages a 'winning aspiration' and suggests taking five simple steps to explore and test strategy.
3 Tarique, I. and Schuler, R., 2014. A typology of talent-management strategies. In: P. Sparrow, H. Scullion and I. Tarique, eds., *Strategic talent management: Contemporary issues in international context*. Cambridge: Cambridge University Press, pp. 177–193.

4 For an introduction to the Shell approach to scenario planning, visit www.shell.com/energy-and-innovation/the-energy-future/scenarios/what-are-scenarios.html (accessed 24.1.2019).

5 See Chamorro-Premuzic, T., 2017. *The talent delusion: Why data, not intuition is the key to unlocking human potential.* London: Piatkus.

6 See Sparrow, P., Scullion, H. and Tarique, I., 2014. Multiple lenses on talent management: Definitions and contours of the field. In: P. Sparrow, H. Scullion and I. Tarique, eds., *Strategic talent management: Contemporary issues in International context.* Cambridge: Cambridge University Press, 36–70.

7 See Bidwell, M., 2011. Paying more to get less: The effects of external hiring versus internal mobility. *Administrative Science Quarterly* 56(3), 369–407.

8 This is referred to as triangulation, originating from navigational techniques, using two points to establish a third.

9 Keller, J.R. and Cappelli, P., 2014. A supply-chain approach to talent management. In: P. Sparrow, H. Scullion and I. Tarique, eds., *Strategic talent management: Contemporary issues in international context.* Cambridge: Cambridge University Press, pp. 117–150.

10 A range of studies point to the low success rate of external hires, for example, Groysberg, Lee and Nanda, 2008; Bidwell, 2011, cited in Keller and Capelli 2014.

11 Many academics have referenced the lack of joined-up thinking between talent (organisationally driven) and career (individually driven), suggesting they are based on different assumptions (e.g. De Vos, A. and Dries, N., 2013). Applying a talent management lens to career management: The role of human capital composition and continuity. *The International Journal of Human Resource Management* 24(9), 1816–1831.

12 For examples, see the writing of Jacob Morgan on the future of work and the importance of the employee experience, www.forbes.com/sites/jacobmorgan/2016/04/22/what-is-employee-experience/#43c69a7a7386 (accessed 26.01.2019).

13 For more information on the Maturity Institute and their tools for measuring Total Stakeholder Value (TSV) including OMINEX, visit their website www.hrmaturity.com/ (accessed 30.01.2019).

14 See the excellent book, Herriot, P. and Pemberton, C., 1995. *New deals: The revolution in managerial careers.* New York: John Wiley & Son Ltd.

15 Rousseau, D., 1995. *Psychological contracts in organizations: Understanding written and unwritten agreements.* Thousand Oaks: Sage Publications.

16 For example, the findings of Low, C. H., Bordia, P. and Bordia, S., 2016. What do employees want and why? An exploration of employees' preferred psychological contract elements across career stages. *Human Relations* 69(7), 1457–1481.

17 Silzer, R. and Church, A., 2010. Identifying and assessing high potential talent: Current organizational practices. In: R. Silzer and B. Dowell, eds., *Strategy driven talent management: A leadership imperative.* San Francisco: Jossey-Bass, 213–280.

18 A recent article highlighted the risk that many talent management processes and tools are being adopted with little concern for their effectiveness or added value. Rotol, C. T., Church, A. H., Adler, S., Smither, J. W., Colquitt, A. L., Shull, A. C., Paul, K. B. and Foster, G., 2018. Putting an end to bad talent management: A call to action for the field of industrial and organizational psychology. *Industrial and Organizational Psychology.* Cambridge University Press 11(2), 176–219.

19 These findings have been found a number of times, that it is perception of the processes rather than the process itself that needs to be the focus of attention. There is often a discrepancy between how processes were intended to be implemented and how they actually end up happening. It is the actual practice, not the intention, that has the impact. For relevant articles, see Nishii, L. H., Lepack, D. P. and Schneider, B., 2008. Employee attributions of the "why" of HR practices: Their effects on employee attitudes and behaviors, and customer satisfaction. *Personnel Psychology* 61(3), 503–545. Or Thunnissen, M., 2016. Talent management: For what, how and how well? An empirical exploration of talent management in practice. *Employee Relations* 38(1), 57–72.

5   HR as liberators

Introduction

The Talent Compass has shown how talent liberation can be applied in practice. We are now going to explore this in more detail, with chapters successively examining the role of key stakeholders (HR, leaders, and individuals) in creating a new mindset around talent. The focus of this chapter is on HR as liberators. If you are in HR, what role can (and perhaps should) you play to liberate more talent to increase competitive advantage? We start by looking at the role, drawing on research data and our own interviews with CEOs to suggest why and how the HR function needs to evolve to meet future challenges. The rest of the chapter explores the implications of such a change in the HR role related to talent. Providing practical examples and challenging questions, we focus particularly on four areas for action, as illustrated in Figure 5.1: applying the principles of evidence-based decision making; broadening the ecosystem; adding value through formal process and promoting a positive talent climate. We recognise that there are other 'hot topics' and aspects of HR's talent role which also merit discussion (such as assessment and data analytics). However, we have chosen to focus on the areas which we see as particularly pertinent to our talent liberation approach rather than more general topics. Although written particularly through an HR lens, this chapter should make interesting reading for anyone in a leadership position. You can use it to create an agenda for conversations with your people team, or you can use it to improve your own practice.

Redefining the role

Human Capital is recognised as a key intangible asset of every organisation. Indeed some organisations such as Google, Apple and Microsoft have few assets other than their people and their culture. Yet human capital does not appear on the balance sheet of most businesses. There is a desire to change this, but until an agreed protocol for accounting for human capital is developed, we need to find the best way we can to demonstrate the value of human capital in our own organisations and of using business data to identify the risks and solutions[1]

Figure 5.1 Actions for HR as liberators of talent

The changing role of HR has long been discussed, and many in the professional community would say that they are now engaged in more strategic work and fewer administrative tasks than they were historically. However, the evidence is not so convincing. The eighth study of the HR function conducted by Edward Lawler and John Boudreau at the Center for Effective Organisations[2] made depressing reading. Tracking a variety of strategies and trends, they concluded that in the past 20 years, there has been little change in how HR directors spend their time and that theirs often remains an administrative function. They identified that few HR executives operate in the strategic space or use evidence to lead debates on organisational capability, change and performance. A strategic role offers the biggest opportunity for added value and impact on organisational performance. Such a role requires a significant shift in mindset, away from 'management' and 'partner' towards being a proactive business leader, modelled on professional services firms to improve productivity across the organisation.[3] HR has been described as at an 'inflexion point'[4] in its contribution to organisations, particularly given the changes in the world of work discussed in Chapter 2. So what role should HR be taking on, and how does that link to the premises of talent liberation? Our conversations with CEOs and non-executive directors have given us helpful insight into what business leaders say they really want from HR. The themes are consistent with messages delivered from major consultancies and academic research.[5] Business leaders want and need HR functions that are fully integrated with the business, driving strategy and supporting data-driven decisions about people. They are not there yet.

For example, Alistair Cox, CEO of global recruitment firm Hays Plc, described the need for HR to be alongside the CFO as the 'Chief Lieutenants' of the CEO. He looks to his HR function to be a disrupter, to be controversial and to challenge the business in how to create and drive value for the short and long term. Similarly, Simon Downing, chairman at the fast-growing technology firm Civica, expects HR to be leading the debate on the future of the organisation. Drawing parallels between the evolution of HR and the evolution of other functions such as Finance, he describes HR transitioning from systems and control towards strategic added value. This, he suggests, can be achieved through outsourcing the administrative side of the function and concentrating on understanding specific challenges that impact short-, medium- or long-term business performance. Once these challenges are identified, pragmatic and commercially based solutions should be suggested. He expects HR to be proactive in this – not to wait to be asked but to bring it to the table. Whilst being advocates of the power of technology to support HR, Alistair and Simon also caution about unintended consequences of implementing technological solutions. For example, they describe the risk of selection being so automated that it creates clones or disengages the potential recruit, thus reinforcing the importance of retaining unique human skills described in Chapter 2.

So how should the role of HR evolve? We have summarised our review of the literature[6] and our conversations with stakeholders as five fundamental themes of the HR role going forwards (see Table 5.1).

Interestingly, further research by John Boudreau suggests that one group of HR leaders is fulfilling the role in a fundamentally different way. These are the people who move into HR from other functional roles.[7] Their actions are focused on the bigger picture outcome of business results rather than the contributing people outcomes such as recruitment or retention. They achieve this by looking across the organisation, being curious about how things impact each other, using data to start dialogue and being willing to try things out, to take risks rather than play things safe. These HR leaders are of the view that HR can be one of the most impactful roles in an organisation.

Relating this broader change in HR role to talent, we suggest that the Talent Compass provides an ideal tool which drives links between organisational goals/challenges and talent strategy. More specifically, we see four areas of action for HR to take in order to unlock the potential to be a liberator of talent rather than a curator or gatekeeper.

Table 5.1 HR role for the future

Understand the organisation	Build a picture of the specific challenges your organisation faces and the capabilities you are likely to need for short- and long-term success in terms of people, culture and process. Develop solutions that fit this context. (The Talent Compass can help you with this.)
Focus on outcomes	Concentrate effort on the bigger picture goals. Don't get sidetracked into activities which add little value or could be outsourced. (For example, are succession plans delivering the outcome you need, or are they being completed because they're part of the annual calendar?)
Support decisions through evidence	Create commercially based business cases, looking at the impact on internal and external stakeholders and providing information to help internal clients to make good decisions. Close liaison with the finance function can support identification of financial benefits. (Some guidance is given in the next section.)
Take a broader view	Think long term and recognise that the boundaries of the organisation are wider than those employed within it, so be connected to what is going on outside the organisation, including looking at the long-term needs and the wider talent ecosystem (which is explored in more detail later).
Be proactive	Don't wait to be invited or asked to investigate a particular issue, but work with other functions to pre-empt the issues and be willing to try things out.

Using evidence to improve outcomes

According to the Center for Evidence Based Management,[8] evidence-based practice focuses on helping managers to adopt a more critical approach to decision making, using 'best available evidence' to improve the quality of decisions rather than relying on received wisdom or 'best practice'. The evidence used may come from scientific literature, internal organisational data, input from stakeholders and the professional insights of practitioners. Multiple sources are likely to improve the quality of the information and hence decisions. They suggest six steps to taking an evidence-based approach:

1 Asking: translating a practical issue or problem into an answerable question
2 Acquiring: systematically searching for and retrieving the evidence
3 Appraising: critically judging the trustworthiness and relevance of the evidence
4 Aggregating: weighing and pulling together the evidence
5 Applying: incorporating the evidence into the decision-making process
6 Assessing: evaluating the outcome of the decision taken

Source: Reproduced with permission from Barends, E. and Rousseau, D. M., 2018. *Evidence-based management: How to use evidence to make better organizational decisions.* Kogan Page Publishers.

The case for using an evidence-based approach is compelling. As brilliantly illustrated in Daniel Kahneman's bestselling book, *Thinking, fast and slow*,[9] personal intuition and judgement is tempting but ultimately unreliable. Furthermore, evidence obtained through practice in other organisations may not apply, and as we have seen, there can be a disconnect between academic research and organisational practice. Within this book we have tried to contribute input from scientific literature and professional insights of practitioners. However, this needs to be supplemented by internal data and input from stakeholders to ensure it is appropriately applied to your context. The growth in availability of internal organisational data is creating challenges for HR professionals who report feeling ill-equipped to navigate their way through data and statistics.[10] Our purpose here is to signpost some helpful resources to support you to take better evidence-based approaches to your talent data.

There can be challenges with any or all of the six steps for evidence-based practice. Here are some particular difficulties that we have encountered with clients when encouraging an evidence-based approach to talent:

- *Asking the right question.* Paradoxically, you may need to ask lots of questions before you can identify the ones you want to concentrate on. So, for example, you may discuss the Talent Compass with stakeholders. In one organisation, this may then translate as questions regarding the definition and assessment of High Potential. In another organisation, this may indicate a focus on how to increase retention of people with key skills. Each question will require different probing questions to help to unlock the underlying problem.
- *Focusing on the outcome, not the output.* The evidence being acquired needs to relate to what matters for the business, the outcomes rather than the outputs of an intervention. For example, an appropriate outcome measure of training is the impact on productivity and engagement. However, an output measure may be the number of training hours or the level of course satisfaction. It can be difficult to identify appropriate outcome measures as there are often many other influences (such as the influence of the line manager).
- *Drawing conclusions from data.* There is much talk and investment in 'big data' and the use of statistics to inform decisions. Economist Alec Levenson went as far as to say, 'there often is an inverse correlation between fancy statistics and business insights'.[11] For example, when delving into the data, statistical correlations are often presented as if they showed causality,[12] and case studies often present data indicating business improvement, but financial performance is not measured. Rather, it is people's *perceptions* of benefits.

The Center for Evidence Based Management website has many practical examples, case studies and resources.[13] We have also found the 'Valuing your Talent Framework'[14] very helpful for illustrating how to apply an evidence-based approach. Drawing on a collaboration across professional bodies representing perspectives on business, HR, finance and social challenges, they suggest a common framework for understanding, measuring and reporting on the value that people contribute to the organisation. The framework distinguishes between activities (such as performance management and recruitment), outputs (such as engagement and leadership capability) and outcomes (such as organisational culture, performance and productivity). These distinctions are important to help ensure that there is always a clear outcome in mind rather than focusing on the activity as an end in itself. Suggested internal metrics are also given, creating a valuable resource for exploring potential sources of internal data. For example, they suggest that a measure of organisational agility and resilience could be evidence of successful change in line with business objectives.

We recognise that it can be difficult to build confidence in taking a more evidence-based approach. Indeed it can feel that it will slow things down, create unnecessary complications, and confirm what you already know. But the risks are high with any people or talent intervention, and an evidence-based approach is all about increasing (not guaranteeing) the chances of success.

Broadening the talent ecosystem

In Chapter 2, we saw how the changes in work are impacting macro and internal structures of organisations as well as career expectations. Increasingly, organisations are looking at alternative ways to access the talent they need, considering when it makes more sense to 'borrow' talented people (through secondments, projects, contracting or outsourcing) instead of 'buying' (recruiting) them.[15] Accessing different sources of talented people in different ways is a crucial way to overcome the mindset of scarcity and replace it with the first premise of talent liberation that 'talent isn't as scarce as we think'. It is also an essential ingredient of providing a responsive talent strategy to deliver on premise four, to 'be responsive to changing talent needs'. According to Jon Younger and Michael Kearns, there are five key benefits that executives are seeking when they look to access talented people without necessarily recruiting them:

---

1   Leverage the increased availability of external expertise
2   Reduce cost
3   Avoid adding permanent headcount
4   Increase the speed of getting things done
5   Challenge internal thinking and assumptions with new ideas from outside

Source: From 'The Future of Teams: Managing the blended workforce' White Paper by toptal.[16]

It appears that this 'borrow' approach (also referred to as agile talent) is creating a fundamental shift in organisational makeup such that in the future half the workforce in many organisations may be people who are not traditional, permanent employees. Consequently, any talent strategy needs to apply as much to the nontraditional workers as it does the core employees. HR needs to be clear on how to attract, select, deploy, develop and engage these people and integrate them with workers who may have a more traditional employed relationship with the organisation. However, evidence from the Human Resource Excellence research indicates that many HR professionals currently have little involvement in providing direction and services for such workers.[17]

This raises a number of questions for HR. Here we focus on three. First, what is your talent ecosystem, and how do you strengthen it? Second, how do you decide on when to borrow and when to buy? Third, when you do engage the services of a nontraditional worker, how do you make it successful for both parties and for other employees?

- *What is your talent ecosystem?* According to the Mercer (2018) Global Talent Trends Study, there are five parts to a talent ecosystem (the sources of supply that are considered in the Talent Compass). They identified (1) internal employees, (2) partnership arrangements where talent is exchanged with other companies, (3) freelance workers of independent talent, (4) crowdsourced and (5) 'co-opetition', where there is collaboration with the competition for mutual benefit. Whatever the source of the talented people, as previously discussed, it is essential to know who has what skills, what their availability is and what their goals and motivations are. Increasingly this knowledge is provided by technology, be it existing HR platforms or bespoke talent solutions that provide a joined-up picture of internal and other forms of talent.[18] Other organisations use existing platforms to identify and connect with talented people. For example, social media platforms are increasingly used by workers looking for opportunities and by companies looking to find people with certain skills, and there are a number of sites dedicated to matching people and work.[19] In addition to the technology solutions, many organisations build relationships with brokers, such as recruitment firms and consultancies, relying on them to have the visibility of external talent and to provide the appropriate introductions.
- *How do you decide when to borrow and when to buy?* This decision will be driven by weighing up the answers to a number of questions about the suitability of the five different parts of the talent ecosystem outlined earlier. For example, how generic versus specialist are the skills? How unique is the context in which the skills are needed? How long will you need access to people with these skills, knowledge and experience? Based on conversations with clients and talent partners (such as recruitment agencies, freelancers and outsourcers), plus a review of some relevant literature,[20] we have developed a simple framework to help your decision making on when to borrow,

buy or build. This can be found in section C of the Toolkit and Resources at the end of the book.

- *How do you make the relationship successful?* Accessing the resource is only part of the challenge. The relationship needs to work, not only for the business but also for the worker (delivering on the fifth premise of talent liberation that success depends on partnership between the organisation and the people). In some ways, the aligning process for talent outside the organisation is simpler than it is for internal people as the contract, or deal, is often more transactional. However, as this type of work increases and people who are not traditionally employed make up a larger percentage of the workforce, there is a need to think about the nature of the relationship more broadly. To date there has been minimal research on the impact of the shift to a talent ecosystem approach. However, a number of risks have been identified,[21] and there is particular concern regarding fairness and potential for people to be disadvantaged by working in the gig economy.[22] Other writers and reports[23] have looked at how to help people and organisations to thrive as talent is accessed by organisations in more ways.

- Think what motivates your agile workforce to want to work with you – and design assignments that provide this. For example, lots of freelancers want interesting and varied projects. Think how you can package work to provide appealing opportunities.
- Be willing to operate at pace. Agile workers may not wait for you to make a decision.
- Be clear what you are offering and make sure you deliver on it.
- Include your agile workforce as part of your talent strategy and your people discussions. For example, how can you better attract and deploy them? What other skills do they have that you could use?
- Remember that the basics of good management still apply. These include meaningful work, clear metrics of expectations with feedback and a relationship where people feel valued.

AECOM is a global infrastructure business, regularly featured as one of *Fortune* magazine's 'world's most admired companies'. They needed to build an external, on-demand workforce to cater to the increasing variability of their workload. They wanted to create and build a shared, searchable, trusted and live contingent database, developing a strong relationship between a high-quality pool of contractors and AECOM. The project looked to create a more holistic and long-term approach when engaging and maintaining an external talent pool. They partnered with Adepto to use their platform to build a network of high-quality external talented people and to establish a presence within the contractor/contingent market and strengthen the relationship with known talented people. The purpose was to reduce over-reliance on agencies and external recruiters and better manage costs by scaling up workforces as needed. The results included a strong contractor brand known as 'AECOM Link', a network of over 450 external contractors, positive candidate feedback about the opportunity to maintain their profile and connect directly with the organisation and growth to 18% contingent working towards a target of 25%.

Case study reproduced with permission, provided by Adepto.[24]

Adding value through formal process

We have already described some of the challenges of formal processes of talent management. Indeed it has been suggested that some of the processes, such as succession planning, are a legacy of a bygone age when 90% of positions were filled internally rather than the current 33%.[25] However, as we have discussed, formal process has a part to play as long as it is purposeful, fits with the culture and delivers the desired outcomes. To paraphrase the sentiment of the Agile HR Manifesto described in Chapter 3, whilst we value the contribution of formal process, we value the informal, adaptive, collaborative and transparent approaches more.

The starting point for adding value through formal processes is to review the appropriate Talent Compass questions. This sets out the aim that '*Our formal processes help the organisation and our people to meet their short and long term goals*'. Based on our experiences and research evidence,[26] we have categorised common formal talent processes under three headings (see Table 5.2).

Table 5.2 Three categories of formal talent process

Foundational	A basic tool or process that is likely to apply to all organisations and (when done well) will contribute to improved business performance through enabling more people to be at their Personal Best.
Simple	Tools that can be readily implemented and are likely to contribute to business performance, but there is less evidence to support these and their appropriateness will depend on the needs of the organisation. These tools may be applied to specific employee groups to help to address particular issues.
Tailored	Specific processes and activities that may be appropriate, depending on the growth/risk issues for the organisation (e.g. as identified in the Talent Compass). There is case study evidence that these processes can add value. However, their value is likely to be context-specific, and implementation is likely to involve a project of some type in order to adapt the tool to the context and to secure buy-in from stakeholders.

Foundational processes

We have identified two specific foundational activities: performance management and executive engagement in talent issues. Research demonstrates the value of ongoing performance management based on feedback, goal setting, development, evaluation and reward. However, the impact of formal processes is often limited by poor feedback skills and a lack of manager buy-in. A focus on improving the quality of feedback (delivery and the way it is received) can greatly increase the effectiveness of talent management. Research suggests that creating a supportive feedback environment, linking feedback to coaching and tailoring the feedback delivery to the recipient's needs can all help improve this vital practice.[27] (We explore this further in the next section of this chapter.) There may also be some benefits of a move away from performance ratings and towards more regular 'check-ins' – if they are skilfully executed.[28]

Board engagement in talent issues is another fundamental for a successful talent strategy. Without it, it is still possible to influence the talent agenda, but the senior role modelling will clearly influence the interest throughout the rest of the organisation.[29] Further, as talent strategy needs to be focused on the future of the organisation, board input and engagement are critical for direction setting and securing investment when needed. Senior team engagement in the talent agenda is heavily influenced by the behaviour and commitment of the CEO, and delivery of talent initiatives is limited if people within the business see that talent is an 'HR'-owned initiative rather than a business issue.[30] In our experience, the questions of the Talent Compass provide a helpful way to instigate conversations to engage and involve the board in shaping the talent strategy.

Simple processes

There are many simple processes that an organisation can adopt. For example, many organisations have processes to advertise internal vacancies, to induct new joins, to provide feedback on performance and to discuss learning and development. Other organisations have developed simple approaches to recognise managers who contribute to others' learning, to provide tools to support self-directed learning and to provide resources to support career self-management. Some of these simple processes may apply to everyone (helping them to be at their Personal Best); others may be targeted at a specific group such as those with High Potential. The impact of these programmes is typically not separately evaluated, but feedback from stakeholders indicates that they have been well received. For example, one client we work with has helped High Potential leaders to set up an online network (using 'yammer')[31] to share learning, seek support and signpost additional resources. This is low investment, but is well perceived by the High Potential leaders and anecdotally is encouraging them to collaborate more. Another organisation we work with has recently trained internal career mentors to be available for career conversations with anyone who would value some support.

Tailored processes

Other formal processes may be more complex and will clearly need to be tailored to the organisation's needs and the outcomes being sought. Many books on talent management describe these processes through the lens of the employee lifecycle, starting with attraction, selection and recruitment and progressing through to development and retention. However, as previously discussed, success will not be achieved by simply applying what has worked for others, but rather from an understanding of your organisation and its needs.

Tailored processes may be used to build insight or to manage a risk that has been identified in the Talent Compass. Some sample processes are given in Table 5.3. Further examples can be found in section B of the toolkit, showing Talent Compass sample risks and solutions.

Table 5.3 Tailored processes to build insight and manage risk

Processes to build insight	• Mapping future talent demand • Assessing High Potential leaders and others • Leadership succession plans to identify risks • Key roles' identification and succession plans • Reporting on HR and talent and business performance metrics • Engagement surveys • Understanding individual aspirations
Processes to manage identified risks	• Technical training • Leadership development • Knowledge transfer activities • Processes to facilitate job rotations and internal moves • Attraction and selection processes • Diversity and inclusion programmes • Visibility of career pathways • Building relationships with agencies and other partners • Flexible contracts and ways of working across the talent ecosystem • Well-being initiatives • Transparency of the career deal • Support for career self-management • Reward and recognition of teams

Promoting a positive talent climate

A large (150,000 people-plus) logistics organisation had evidence that they were losing millions of dollars every year in absenteeism and the trend was increasing year on year. The data were irrefutable. They couldn't afford to lose the money, but they took no action. Why? The climate and culture of the organisation meant that they wanted to ignore the problem. They conducted additional research. This showed an even greater annual loss. Eventually action was taken, and line managers were trained to support earlier identification and intervention on mental health and sickness issues. The result? Savings of over $500,000 per year in days lost and people who feel better supported and able to work at their personal best.

Throughout this book we have emphasised the influence of the organisational culture on the whole talent agenda. In our research we have encountered organisations that successfully align their strategic imperative with genuine people investment and a positive culture in which everyone can work towards being their Personal Best. However, many HR professionals we speak with are operating within cultures which, at best, do little to support an agenda of talent liberation and, at worst, actually undermine it. For example, if people's learned behaviour is 'do what the boss says', 'don't make a mistake', 'look after yourself', or 'never give honest feedback', this will be a huge barrier to the success of any talent programme. In the previous chapter we identified three elements of the talent climate: organisation design, organisation culture and observable behaviours. Here we take a different perspective, exploring five things that we observe most often get in the way of a positive talent climate, (see Figure 5.2) with suggestions of how these can be addressed.

Figure 5.2 Barriers to a positive talent climate

1   *Feedback culture.* As suggested in the formal processes described previously, a feedback culture is essential to the success of performance management,[32] yet it is something that many organisations struggle with. This same research, conducted by the Center for Organisational Effectiveness, identifies six dimensions of a performance feedback culture: communication (regarding the importance of feedback and the expectations that managers will deliver honest, effective feedback); training (developing manager skills in providing the feedback); monitoring (capturing data on the delivery of quality feedback); modelling (senior managers receiving and providing quality feedback); rewarding (reinforcing the value of feedback through reward and recognition) and selecting (including the ability to provide feedback as an important selection criteria). The report includes case studies and resources which can be used to assess your organisational practice. The role of leaders in feedback is explored in more detail in the next chapter.

2   *Risk taking.* Many organisations are very risk-averse. Whilst we have been promoting a risk management approach to talent, we are also aware of the unintended consequences of being highly risk averse. Academic research on risk-optimisation in talent (balancing the risk and the opportunity) is limited.[33] However, using practical examples, it is possible to see the benefits of taking a wide view of risk. Some organisations invest considerable time and effort in finding the perfect candidates for vacancies. Individuals recruited are usually external and are already capable of doing the role. They arrive, do the job for a few weeks and quickly feel bored, lacking the head room and stretch to develop. Consequently there is a high turnover of new recruits. Furthermore, there is a huge impact on the existing people. Internal candidates know that they might not be quite ready for the role, but without being given a chance to prove themselves, they see their career development opportunities being blocked. Consequently, despite loving working in the organisation, they are left feeling that they will need to leave to further their career. The organisation is wasting time, money, effort and goodwill, all because they are focused on one risk (the risk of not having the best possible person in the role) and not looking at the other risks associated with their external recruitment, including the high failure rate[34] and the impact on the existing team. A further element of risk is the desire to look for new recruits that match existing high performers. This risks missing the opportunities and fresh perspectives that people with disruptive talent can bring. Taking a wider view of risk and exploring unintended consequences can create a different assessment of the pros and cons of different options, leading to better decisions (or actions to mitigate the negative effect of the decisions).

3   *Not my job.* Managers typically describe developing their people as an interference, something which eats up too much time and gets in the way

of doing the technical or functional part of the role.[35] A. G. Lafley, the celebrated CEO of Procter & Gamble (2000–2010) was quoted as spending between a third and half of his time developing talent.[36] He clearly saw it as an integral part of his job. This is consistent with other findings that suggest that in many top companies, developing talent is seen as 'everyone's business'.[37] However, HR can be complicit in managers not taking accountability for the people aspects of their role, finding it difficult to let go and empower the managers. As one HR consultant said to us, 'HR just don't trust the line manager; they keep dictating more and more about how people management should be done, so it's not surprising that line managers don't feel any ownership'.

So how do you change it? Research from literature on the devolution of HR to the line gives us some clues.[38] Encouraging managers to take on more of the role involves education, training, role modelling, recognition and support. Supporting systems need to be simple, and the challenges of potential role overload also need to be recognised. These issues are only likely to be fully addressed by working with managers and leaders, understanding the barriers within your own organisation and agreeing how they can best be tackled. The next chapter explores the role of the leader and manager in more detail.

4   *Short-term results.* The focus on short-term results by many organisations limits the extent to which people think long term about their product, market, infrastructure and, of course, their people. This is manifest in many ways. For example, in our research collecting people's career stories, there were numerous examples of people's career moves being blocked because they were too valued in their current role. Whilst this may satisfy the organisation's short-term needs, as with the risk-aversion examples given earlier, there are unintended consequences and potential short- and long-term costs as a result of such decisions. Such a short-term focus creates a dilemma for many line managers who may want to develop and encourage movement of their team, but letting them go could limit their ability to hit targets and impact on bonuses. In our own research, it has been interesting to note that the organisations with the most positive talent cultures are those where there is less pressure to hit the quarterly results, but rather a commitment to long-term, sustainable growth.

It has been suggested that HR, with a continued emphasis on short-term and oversimplified metrics has been complicit in this domination of short-term thinking.[39] So the first action that you can take is to role model a longer-term view, applying the 'broader perspective' identified as part of the redefined HR role. This can involve different conversations with managers and leaders, exploring the questions in the Talent Compass to balance the needs of short- and long-term talent requirements.

5   *Lack of transparency*. We have already mentioned the challenges of lack of transparency regarding talent management (chapters 1 and 4). This lack of transparency can work both ways, with organisations failing to disclose their assessments and plans for individuals and, likewise, individuals playing a game by giving expected responses regarding their aspirations rather than being honest. Inevitably, this undermines trust and makes it more difficult to create a positive talent climate where there can be a genuine matching of individual and organisational goals. Indeed it has to be recognised that there is a risk of greater transparency as it may identify a lack of alignment between what both parties want; hence, matching may not be possible.[40] However, our research has indicated that individuals want greater transparency from the organisation, particularly with regard to the career deal and 'how to get on round here'. Such transparency is likely to support career self-management and encourage shared ownership for personal and career development, which both help a positive talent climate. Whilst some HR people are cautious to share data from succession plans or lists of High Potentials, providing greater clarity of the career deal is relatively low risk. Indeed this can be considered an ethical matter and a key part of the employer brand and psychological contract.

6   *Individual over team*. Premise two of talent liberation is that high performance is a result of teams as well as individuals. It is therefore important to explore how the different contributions of teams and individuals are recognised and enabled within the organisation. This is particularly relevant given the changes in internal structures that were described in Chapter 2. Often with organisations, there is a language regarding the importance of teams, but all of the stories, accolades and rewards focus on individual contributions. Teamwork could be more explicitly reinforced and supported. Similarly, despite compelling evidence that high trust between team members contributes to high performance,[41] few organisations coach and support teams to quickly build trust.

As you find ways to create change on these six barriers to a positive talent climate, it can be helpful to apply an agile approach. You may want to start small, to experiment and learn and to involve others in your journey. Finding existing good practice within the organisation is a great way of exploring what might work and engaging a community of people around a common goal. Some insights from marketing can be helpful in considering how to influence the culture. In particular, we have used the work of Jonah Berger on 'Contagious Communication'[42] to help us to work with clients to influence the talent climate. Examples include rewarding excellent internal coaches with a gold-coloured lanyard that created social currency, encouraging people to engage emotionally by publicly thanking the people who had helped them to develop their career and sharing stories of people who had moved across functional boundaries and people who had progressed within the organisation.

Reflections

This chapter has focused on the role of HR professionals as liberators of talent. Using the Talent Compass as a starting point, the emerging role of HR has been explored, showing how the role has perhaps not evolved as much as we would like to think. The importance of deep understanding of your organisation has been shown. It is not appropriate to take 'best practice' from other places. Any actions need to be clearly related to your own strategy, context and culture. In many ways, this makes the HR role far more challenging, but with that comes the opportunity for more influence and interest. However, it is suggested that this influence should be based on evidence. The evidence may emerge from different sources, and it is important to be pragmatic, but intuition alone is not a sound source for judgement.

This chapter has then explored the role of HR in progressing three particular themes from this book. First, we looked in more detail at how the talent ecosystem extends beyond the traditional boundaries of the organisation. The focus here was on how and when to buy, build or borrow talent and how to support the success of that decision. Second, whilst our focus was not on formal talent management processes, we do recognise their value, and consequently we suggested some of the processes that can support the elements of the Talent Compass. We have looked at some foundation processes that are likely to help all organisations as well as some tailored activities that will depend on the strategic aims and identified risks. Finally we explored some important dimensions associated with promoting a positive talent climate. We focused on how HR can encourage change in feedback culture, risk taking, manager accountability, transparency, taking a longer-term perspective and valuing team as well as individual.

- What role do you play in your organisation? Are you leading the debate?
- How can you further build your organisational knowledge?
- What are the outcomes that are most important for you to focus on? How are you measuring impact on these?
- How can you better use evidence to support decision making for you and your stakeholders?
- How can you consistently take a broader view?
- How wide is your talent ecosystem?
- How do you decide when to buy, build or borrow talent?
- What impact do your formal processes have?
- How do you need to supplement, adapt or change them to support your talent plan?
- How does your current culture and climate influence talent liberation?

- How is the talent climate experienced differently by different groups (e.g. High Potentials, people with strategically important skills)?
- How can you influence the talent climate?
- What actions will you take to evolve your role?

Notes

1 For more information on assessing human capital and total value see reports and examples by Ernst and Young, for example, www.ey.com/Publication/vwLUAssets/ey-ccass-total-value-a-broader-vision/$FILE/ey-ccass-total-value-a-broader-vision.pdf (accessed 18.02.2019).
2 Lawler III, E.E. and Boudreau, J.W., 2018. *Human resource excellence: An assessment of strategies and trends.* Redwood City, CA: Stanford University Press.
3 Ulrich, D. and Dulebohn, J.H., 2015. Are we there yet? What's next for HR? *Human Resource Management Review, 25*(2), pp. 188–204.
4 See page 3 Sparrow, P. and Cooper, C.L. eds., 2017. *A research agenda for human resource management.* Cheltenham, UK: Edward Elgar Publishing.
5 For example https://assets.kpmg/content/dam/kpmg/ca/pdf/2018/11/the-future-of-hr-2019.pdf or https://www2.deloitte.com/us/en/pages/human-capital/articles/future-of-hr.html (accessed 30.06.2019).
6 In particular we have drawn on the following articles/books to inform our summary of the future role of HR. Cappelli, P., 2015. Why we love to hate and what HR can do about it. *Harvard Business Review, 93*(7/8), pp. 54–61. Hesketh, A., July 2014. Valuing your talent: Managing the value of your talent, a new framework for human capital measurement. Joint research report by the CIPD, UKCES, CMI, CIMA and RSA, www.cipd.co.uk/Images/managing-the-value-of-your-talent-a-new-framework-for-human-capital-measurement_2014_tcm18-9266.pdf (accessed 18.02.2019). Lawler and Boudreau, 2018. Sparrow and Cooper, eds., 2017. Ulrich and Dulebohn, 2015.
7 For more information on this research, visit www.visier.com/clarity/hr-leadership-lessons-non-traditional-chros/ (accessed 08.02.2019).
8 For more information about the Center and for access to resources, visit their website, www.cebma.org/ (accessed 18.02.2019).
9 Kahneman, D. and Egan, P., 2011. *Thinking, fast and slow* (Vol. 1). New York: Farrar, Straus and Giroux.
10 Angrave, D., Charlwood, A., Kirkpatrick, I., Lawrence, M. and Stuart, M., 2016. HR and analytics: Why HR is set to fail the big data challenge. *Human Resource Management Journal, 26*(1), pp. 1–11.
11 Alec Levenson is Economist and Senior Research Scientist at the Center for Effective Organizations, Marshall School of Business, University of Southern California. For the full blog, visit www.analyticsinhr.com/blog/interview-alec-levenson-people-analytics/
12 Hesketh, A., 2017. Architectures of value: Moving leaders beyond analytics and big data. In: *A research agenda for human resource management.* Cheltenham, UK: Edward Elgar Publishing.
13 Resources and tools, including case studies and slide shares can be found at www.cebma.org/resources-and-tools/ (accessed 18.02.2019).
14 Hesketh, 2014.
15 The term 'borrow or buy' is 'borrowed' from the Mercer 2018 Global Talent Trends Study.
16 For more information on the work of Jon Younger and Michael Kearns visit https://bs-uploads.toptal.io/blackfish-uploads/insights_white_paper_page/content/attachment_file/

attachment/338/Toptal_-_Managing_the_Blended_Workforce-5b45f80ee6c41f48 ab408a1bcdcdc351.pdf (accessed 07.02.2019).

17 For data showing how much HR people apply different HR strategies see pages 37–39 of *Human Resource Excellence* (details as above).

18 Such as the previously mentioned Adepto which offers a platform to locate and access global talent. For more information see www.adepto.com/who-we-are/ (accessed 07.02.2019).

19 The platforms for temporary and casual work are frequently changing and there are many niche providers which focus on particular skills or sectors. However, (as of February 2019) these are some established sites. Peopleperhour: www.peopleperhour.com/; fiverr www. fiverr.com/; Upwork, www.upwork.com/; Amazon M Turk, www.mturk.com/

20 For example, the HR architecture model by Lepak and Snell (1999), which differentiates based on uniqueness and value, plus the attachment map suggested by Rousseau & Wade-Benzoni (1995). Lepak, D.P. and Snell, S.A., 1999. The human resource architecture: Toward a theory of human capital allocation and development. *Academy of Management Review, 24*(1), pp. 31–48. Rousseau, D.M. and Wade-Benzoni, K.A., 1995. *Changing individual – organization attachments: A two-way street.* San Francisco: Jossey-Bass.

21 For example, an ETUI Policy Brief which can be located at https://papers.ssrn.com/sol3/ papers.cfm?abstract_id=2809517 (accessed 07.02.2019).

22 For example, the recent acceptance by courier Hermes that employment benefits such as holiday pay and pay rates should be available to those working on a contract basis, www. bbc.co.uk/news/business-47110934

23 For example, the Mercer Global Talent Trends and PwC report 2019 on 'Secure your future people experience' www.pwc.com/gx/en/people-organisation/pdf/secure-your-future-people-experience-pwc.pdf (accessed 09.05.2019).

24 For more information on Adepto's history, services and case studies, visit their website at www.adepto.com/ (accessed 30.06.2019).

25 Cappelli, 2015.

26 As referenced above.

27 Chawla, N., Gabriel, A.S., Dahling, J.J. and Patel, K., 2016. Feedback dynamics are critical to improving performance management systems. *Industrial and Organizational Psychology.* Cambridge University Press, *9*(2), pp. 260–266.

28 See the article by Alan Colquitt, https://ceo.usc.edu/remove-the-shackles-from-performance-management-so-it-can-serve-your-business/ (accessed 10.02.2019).

29 Stahl, G., Björkman, I., Farndale, E., Morris, S.S., Paauwe, J., Stiles, P., Trevor, J. and Wright, P., 2012. Six principles of effective global talent management. *Sloan Management Review, 53*(2), pp. 25–42.

30 Research conducted with a number of large organisations as part of a Special Interest Group. See the white paper for more details. Sparrow, P., Hird, M. and Balain, S., 2011. *Talent management: Time to question the tablets of stone?* Centre for Performance-led HR White Paper 11/01. Lancaster University Management School.

31 Yammer is an enterprise social network, designed to encourage and support team work, www.yammer.com/logout_landing (accessed 09.05.2019).

32 See the report by Gerald E. Ledford, Jr. Ph.D. and Benjamin Schneider, Ph.D., *Performance Feedback Culture Drives Business Impact.* CEO and i4cp jointly sponsored the study available at https://ceo.usc.edu/files/2018/07/Performance-Feedback-Culture-Drives-Business-Performance-i4cp-CEO-002.pdf (accessed 10.02.2019). See also the McKinsey and Company Survey, www.mckinsey.com/business-functions/organization/our-insights/how-to-create-an-agile-organization (accessed 19.02.2019).

33 Cascio, W.F., Boudreau, J.W. and Church, A.H., 2017. Using a risk-optimisation lens: Maximising talent readiness for an uncertain future. In: *A research agenda for human resource management.* Cheltenham, UK: Edward Elgar Publishing, pp. 55–77.

34 Chamorro-Premuzic, T., 2017. *The talent delusion: Why data, not intuition, is the key to unlocking human potential.* London: Piatkus.

35 Cappelli, 2015.
36 Holstein, W.J., November 2005. Best companies for leaders: P&G's A.G. Lafley is No. 1 for 2005. *The Chief Executive*, pp. 16–20.
37 See the article by Dave Ulrich and Jessica Johnson, on 'How top companies for Leaders Develop and Retain their High Potential Employees', http://rblip.s3.amazonaws.com/Articles/Winning%20Tomorrow%27s%20Talent%20Battle.pdf (accessed 10.05.2019).
38 For example, see a literature review reported in Personnel Review, Intindola, M., Weisinger, J.Y., Benson, P. and Pittz, T., 2017. The evolution of devolution in HR. *Personnel Review*, *46*(8), pp. 1796–1815.
39 For example, see Stone, D.L. and Deadrick, D.L., 2015. Challenges and opportunities affecting the future of human resource management. *Human Resource Management Review*, *25*(2), pp. 139–145; Marchington, M., 2015. Human resource management (HRM): Too busy looking up to see where it is going longer term? *Human Resource Management Review*, *25*(2), pp. 176–187.
40 See Cappelli, P. 2008. Talent management for the twenty-first century. *Harvard Business Review*, *86*(3) pp. 74–81.
41 For example, see De Jong, B.A., Dirks, K.T. and Gillespie, N., 2016. Trust and team performance: A meta-analysis of main effects, moderators, and covariates. *Journal of Applied Psychology*, *101*(8), p. 1134.
42 See resources and links to his articles and books at his website, https://jonahberger.com/ (accessed 10.05.2019).

6 Leaders as liberators

Vince is MD of a successful insurance business, and he is a great example of a talent liberator. The business has a reputation for being different, innovative and ambitious, and this is a good way to describe Vince too. His leadership is based on really knowing his team, treating them like adults, understanding their motivations and working with them to enable them to deliver their best work. Learning and personal responsibility are at the heart of the business, informing how everything happens. Some of this is in the small things. For example, there used to be a dress policy, but Vince said, 'What does it say about our opinion of people if we don't trust them to make the most basic of decisions for themselves (i.e. what to wear)? Besides, I believe people make better decisions when they are comfortable'. Other examples are in the big bets he will take, for example, giving a junior member of the marketing team ownership for a project to develop new, disruptive business models. Vince encourages decisions to be taken by the person best placed to take them (based on knowledge and insight rather than status). For this to work, he's created an environment where people feel safe. If mistakes are made, they are openly discussed, explored and learned from. He also recognises how his actions can unintentionally undermine the ownership of the team. So, for example, he no longer attends trading meetings, which reinforces the message that the people in the room are accountable. Vince has built trusting and transparent relationships with the team, so he's able to have conversations about people's future career options. The business is only 195 people, so he knows that he can't satisfy everyone's career aspirations in the long term. But if and when people are ready to move on, he is supportive, celebrating their contribution and being happy to have created the opportunities for people to learn, develop and progress their career.

Getting here hasn't always been easy. Vince still finds it difficult to give up control, to delegate decisions and let them stick, particularly if they are different from the decisions he would have made. This can be especially hard when things aren't going well and he has to fight the urge to intervene. It has also meant redefining his own role. If you're empowering those around to make the decisions that you used to make, what are you going to do? He sees his role as creating an environment and culture where people coach, develop and challenge each other, helping them to continually build their self-awareness and challenging themselves to do their best. He has also found that some people really don't want to take responsibility. They would rather someone else tell them what to do, and this can be a challenge too. It can mean that the fit between them and the business just isn't going to work.

Despite these challenges, Vince is committed. He describes the prize as huge, with high adaptability, ambition and a top 10% engagement score compared with external benchmarks. Then there is the satisfaction of seeing people step up and do things that they previously thought they could not do, the results of liberating their talent.

Introduction

As we have seen in previous chapters, everyone with responsibility for leading or managing others is at the front line of talent liberation. Ideally they collaborate with other leaders and the HR team to support liberation across the organisation, bringing the competitive advantage that we have discussed. However, when this is not possible, leaders and managers can still have a positive influence on their team and those they interact with. Table 6.1 summarises some of the talent liberation leadership actions explored in previous chapters. Many of these are actions that help you to influence across the organisational system as shown in the Talent Compass.

Within this chapter, we zoom in on how leaders and managers can release individual and team talent. This may cover people within your own team and may also cover people in the wider talent ecosystem who you are working collaboratively with. It may cover any or all of the talent quadrants described in Chapter 1. For example, you could focus on increasing the mean performance level with everyone working at their Personal Best, or you may cover the few who demonstrate particularly High Potential.[1] Using the Talent Compass, you can identify the biggest risks you need to mitigate. However, in general, if your success depends on someone's performance, then it is in your interests to consider how to help them to be the best they can be, and this chapter can help.

Over the years, we have asked hundreds of successful people about their career. We have asked who or what has been most influential in helping them get where they are, in helping them to achieve more of their potential. The question brings a range of responses. Often there is a significant 'in at the deep-end' experience where the person has had to really stretch themselves beyond what they thought they were capable of.[2] One strikingly common theme is the contribution of a significant mentor, manager or helper. This is someone who, just in the classic

Table 6.1 Talent liberation premises and leadership role

Talent challenges	Premise of talent liberation and the role of leaders
Mindset of scarcity	1 **Talent is not as scarce as we think**. Leaders can work to identify hidden sources of potential, to increase everyone's Personal Best and to explore new sources of talent from outside the traditional boundaries of the organisation.
Cult of individual heroes	2 **High performance is a result of teams as well as individuals**. Leaders can role-model and support collaboration, creating an environment where teams can flourish. They can recognise the contribution of teams to competitive advantage and encourage shared learning between teams.
Lack of strategic clarity	3 **We need to be responsive to changing talent needs**. Leaders need to think about the possible future scenarios (including the impact of technology, global and internal structures) and identify the skills they may require for the future. Securing access to diverse talent pools and balancing short- and long-term needs will support greater agility. The Talent Compass provides a tool to capture these needs.
Dominance of formal process	4 **Formal processes are only part of the answer**. Leaders exert a strong influence on the culture. Developing a positive informal talent climate can greatly enhance the impact of formal processes and drive competitive advantage through more people performing at their Personal Best and by developing people with High Potential.
Missing half the story	5 **Success depends on partnership between the organisation and the people**. Leaders are the 'brokers' between the organisation and the individual, helping to find ways where the needs and aspirations of both parties can be met. They need to find ways to personalise the offer to appeal to people with different career aims.

structure of mythological tales, is a guide, helping them to take on the call to adventure, to navigate the challenges or to develop the skills, abilities or resolve to successfully achieve their quest. For example, Steve Jobs referred to Bill Campbell as a mentor; Mark Zuckerberg to Steve Jobs; Bill Gates to Warren Buffet and Richard Branson to Freddie Laker.

For Joy, the manager in her second job was the one who really propelled her career forwards. He took a chance on her, putting her in a role she wasn't really ready for. He was uncompromising in his standards and his belief that she could do it. He was ok at support and very strong on challenge, consistently giving feedback on how she could stretch herself and do more. Through this, she started to see herself differently – as someone with a valuable voice at the senior table. She learnt to use her voice and grew in her confidence and contribution far faster than she would otherwise have done. This manager was a real catalyst for her development.

Combining our research with that of others in the field,[3] this chapter provides a route map for you to become a guide or mentor, to become a brilliant liberator of talent. We know that it can be difficult to see added value from some of the people management activities you have to do, so we want to show how you can integrate talent liberation into your everyday work. Borrowing terminology from Stephen Covey,[4] we're going to introduce you to five habits of highly effective liberators (see Figure 6.1). As we describe these habits, we will share examples of how people have built them into their daily work and the benefits it can bring. Our aim is to inspire you to develop some (or all) of these habits, helping you and those around you spend more time at their Personal Best and developing potential for the future. The payback for these new habits is clear: greater engagement, improved team performance, lower turnover and your enhanced reputation as a leader.[5]

These habits may seem like common sense, and you may believe that you're already demonstrating them. However, the evidence suggests that you may not

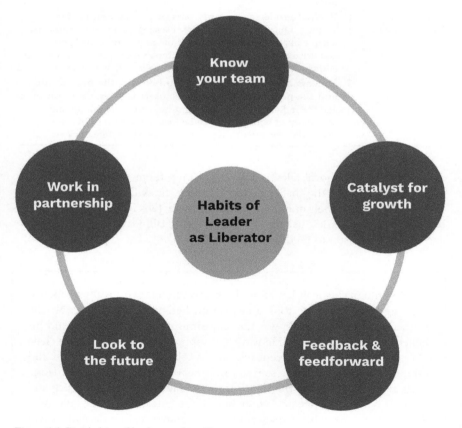

Figure 6.1 Five habits of leader as talent liberator

be as good as you think.[6] The scale of the opportunity to improve was captured in a recent survey conducted by YouGov on behalf of the CIPD.[7] This survey found that 30% of employees felt that they are overqualified for their job and only 12% felt that their organisation inspired them to perform at their best. Relating more specifically to the line manager, 41% of employees said they had only received feedback once or twice in the past 12 months, with 18% saying they didn't get any feedback; 28% indicated that their manager was poor or very poor at discussing their training and development needs with them, and nearly 20% of people suggested that their manager didn't make them feel that their work counted. Furthermore, evidence from a recent LinkedIn Learning report indicated that line manager support and involvement was crucial for successful learning.[8] This raises the question: why are these things not happening? Why, given all of the compelling evidence, do leaders not invest time in these habits? Despite good intentions, all too often, development activities end up low down on the priority list as the type of things that leaders and managers think they will do when they have time. The risk is that this time never materialises, so it ends up being only those who naturally enjoy developing their team who invest time in it.

At an organisational level, this can be addressed through driving greater accountability. The Talent Strategy Group has developed a ten-step 'Accountability ladder' for you to audit the level of accountability that leaders in your organisation have[9]: where leaders take low accountability for development of talented people, there are no consequences; up to a score of 4, where there is cultural pressure to do (or not do) it or up to a 10, where you can be dismissed for lack of action. As a leader, it can be helpful to work through the short- and long-term impact of action and no action to help you to assess the benefits and payback of investing in liberating the talent of your team. Most leaders who engage in this review decide that the investment of time and effort is worth it. As a leader, you can have a direct impact and make sure that your team are reporting positive engagement and feeling enabled to perform at their best.

Habit one: knowing your team

Jeff is an executive director at a global software firm. Over the past few years we've conducted a number of internal talent assessments for members of Jeff's team. Part of this is collecting 360-degree feedback via phone calls, and Jeff is one of the contributors. At the end of the assessment, we catch up with Jeff to discuss the findings and the next steps (before then sharing it with the team member). Jeff's assessment is always spot-on. He knows his people inside out. He sees them all as individuals, not employees or staff. He understands their core strengths and the things they find more difficult. He knows their motivations, and he sees strengths in them that they don't recognise themselves. He understands how to get the best out of them, when to challenge and when to keep out of it. He doesn't use sophisticated tools or frameworks, but he does spend time thinking about his people and talking to them, so he gets under the surface of what they're like. He can't imagine operating in any other way. The way he sees it, he spends time thinking about his customers, his product and his strategy, so of course he wants to spend time thinking properly about his people. He wants to make sure he can always look himself in the mirror and know that he's done the right thing by his team, no matter how difficult.

What do you know about your team? Your aim is to develop insights to maximise people's talents across all of the quadrants so you can help everyone to be at their Personal Best in the short and long term and to create an environment where you can identify and develop people with High Potential. Through our coaching and assessment work, we have prioritised four questions which help to capture insights about individual performance and potential. These questions provide most insight when they are based not just on your observations, but also on conversations with the team member and ideally some of the people they regularly work with (for example in the context of 360 feedback). The core questions are shown in bold in Table 6.2, with additional probing questions listed beneath.

Table 6.2 Knowing your team: questions for leaders

At their best	**What is this person like at their best?**
	• What are they doing?
	• What impact do they have?
	• What seem to be the common patterns or triggers for this?
	• How much of the time do they spend at their best?
At their worst.	**What is this person like at their worst?**
	• What are they doing?
	• What impact do they have?
	• What seem to be the common patterns or triggers for this?
	• How much of the time do they spend at their worst?
Development	**What needs to change to help them to spend more time at their best and less time at their worst?**
	• What would the impact of this be?
	• How could this change be enacted?
In the future	**What could this person do in the future?**
	• What do they aspire to in the future in their current role or in a different role?
	• What can I imagine them doing better or differently?

Asking these as open questions should help you to build a picture of when this person is most motivated, when they are 'on a roll' and what the short- and long-term development priorities are. It will also help you to understand if there are any gaps between how you perceive them and how they see themselves. In approaching this, it is important to be aware that you may hold unconscious biases.[10] These biases may influence what you see, what opportunities you give your team members and how you draw insights about their performance and potential. Seeking input from others can help you to develop a rounded and fair assessment of the team member.

Using the four core questions will help you to identify anyone you think has High Potential. This is when you can start being a talent spotter or talent scout,[11] identifying people who seem to have the motivation, the social skills and the capability to develop into roles which the organisation has identified as being particularly important. These people may then receive additional development support or have their development tracked, depending on any formal organisational approaches which may exist.

Building these insights will be easier if you have a trusting relationship with your team members, one where you can both be honest. This has been referred to as a *'real relationship'* characterised by closeness, support, a focus on how people feel as well as what is objectively achieved and ideally a genuine knowledge and care for the other person.[12] Without this, the information your team member shares may be based on what they think they *should* say rather than what they really think. If you are not getting a truthful picture, there is a risk that you will act on incomplete or inaccurate data, which will not bring you the intended benefits. Our research has provided many examples of team members playing the game. For example, they may indicate that they want to change roles and are willing to be globally mobile. However, they may really be looking for more stretch and challenge in their current role. If you feel that your relationship is not yet trusting enough, then start by spending time talking to them; finding out more about their career history, their likes and dislikes and sharing information on yourself. Getting to know your team is about having great conversations.

Habit two: catalyst for growth

'My manager was brilliant at getting the best from me. It wasn't always clear or planned, but I was learning all the time, and I was constantly being given more accountability. He recognised my potential and opened up a new world of opportunities'.

Meera, Executive Assistant, professional services

'She was pushing and challenging me all the time to be better. Sometimes it was uncomfortable, and I was out of my comfort zone, but she was there, giving me new opportunities, supporting me to be my best, to unlock my skills'.

James, Sales Manager, FMCG

'I try to measure my success by what I have been able to positively impact on in terms of the organisation and also what impact I have had on talented individuals to help unlock their potential. There are some that I have had a positive impact on, and they are now outstandingly successful. The actions I did were around supporting them in their development, giving them the opportunity. I feel pleased if I played a small part – and this is a key part of my leadership role and of my satisfaction in it. Growing talent to help fulfil potential helps the individual, and as a side benefit, it helps the employer'.

Chris, Technical Manager, international engineering

As we have seen, learning and development opportunities are considered a key driver of engagement. With the increasing popularity of the 70:20:10 model[13] (70% from challenging assignments; 20% from developmental relationships and 10% from coursework and training), there is a clear expectation that most of this learning will take place on the job, with the line manager taking a lead role. Supporting this learning is not an optional extra. It is important across the talent quadrants, helping everyone to be their Personal Best as the demands of the job evolve, and it is particularly important for those who want to move into other roles as there are fewer 'stepping stone' roles for people to develop their skills. For example, 20 years ago, a first experience of line management was likely to involve one or two people reporting to you, giving you the opportunity to develop and hone your skills. However, with the work changes described in Chapter 2, many first–line management positions are now based on project work rather than direct reporting relationships, and first 'manager' roles frequently have at least six direct reports. This is a tough challenge for someone with no previous line management experience. Leaders need to help their people to fill these experience gaps.

So how can you fulfil this? How can you be a great developer of your team alongside delivering on your tasks? We see these two demands as complementary. The more you invest in the development of your team, the better engaged they will be and the better skilled at completing their role, which will increase your productivity. Developing your people is never likely to seem urgent. However, scheduling time to invest in this is likely to reduce the need to firefight and to have urgent demands.[14] Intellectually, most managers understand this, but as we have seen previously, there is not enough action. So we want to show how learning and development opportunities can be built into every interaction you have without creating substantial new demands. Creating learning opportunities is about how you work with your team. It does not need to be time consuming.

Table 6.3 Leader as catalyst for growth: everyday learning opportunities

Projects	Projects provide an important opportunity for new learning experiences and stretch beyond the normal day job, keeping people stimulated and engaged as well as preparing them for future opportunities.
Team meetings	Typical team meetings may be transactional and focused on business updates and short-term problem solving, not longer-term issues. However, team meetings can become a critical source of learning if this is consciously part of the purpose and the agenda.
One-to-one updates or check-ins	Most leaders meet with their direct reports at least monthly. This is an important time to work through some of the 'Know your team' questions outlined earlier. You can also use it to follow up on any development actions you have agreed, making sure they are still on the agenda rather than waiting until the annual review.
Coaching	Coaching is recognised as a key development tool, and many leaders will be informally or formally coaching their team. To make the most of this, it is helpful to link it to specific development goals. The well-known GROW acronym[15] is a helpful way to structure your coaching.
Big bets	People will only get their 'in at the deep end' experiences if someone will take a bet on them. This involves being willing to put them into a role a bit early or to give them a very stretching project. There is some risk in doing this, but also risk in not doing it.
Nudge	Nudge[16] is an approach to influencing behaviour through positive reinforcement and triggers, making it more likely that people will choose the desired option. Widely used in politics and public health, it can also be applied to encourage ongoing learning.

The approach you take may be planned as part of structured development or may include ad-hoc opportunities. The learning could relate to any aspect of the role, for example, functional or technical knowledge, commercial skills and understanding, interpersonal skills, political insights, leadership or management skills. Some simple opportunities are introduced in Table 6.3, with some examples and questions provided in section D of the Tools and Resources at the end of the book.

Habit three: feeding back and feeding forward

A 2018 report by the Institute for Corporate Productivity (i4cp) and the Center for Effective Organizations (CEO)[17] concluded that a strong performance feedback culture can lead to improved individual and organisational performance. A strong feedback culture is supported by training, communication, modelling and rewarding, demonstrating commitment to the importance and value of ongoing feedback. Leaders need to be consistently providing 'high-quality, developmentally oriented feedback'. This is consistent with findings from their other research, which underlines that within high-performance organisations, leaders are the developers of talent.

The power of feedback has been a consistent message in previous chapters where we have explored how to develop a feedback culture. Whether in the world of work, sport, the arts or entertainment, feedback is recognised as a crucial element of learning, helping people to achieve their potential. When combined with feedforward (looking ahead at how improvements can be made), there is an opportunity for clear actions to be identified that will help future performance and learning. However, despite recognition of the importance and value of feedback, it's something that many people struggle to deliver,[18] and many organisations are poorly set up to support it, with inadequate formal appraisal processes and little else. We've coached many managers and leaders through the difficult emotional challenge of delivering both praise and tough feedback. Both are important, but it can feel very alien and uncomfortable, which often leaves things unsaid with a predictable effect on performance: nothing changes.

There are many models of feedback that can help people to plan and deliver it in a clear and consistent way. However, before getting on to the feedback itself, it's worth thinking through the receiving person's mindset and likely response. Some people are very open to feedback and approach it from a growth mindset.[19] They see all feedback as a helpful way to build self-awareness and to understand their impact, what they do well and how they can make improvements. However, people who display more of a fixed mindset are likely to become defensive when they feel they are being criticised. They will try to find flaws in the feedback and to demonstrate why it's not accurate. Therefore, it is helpful to create an environment where people are used to receiving feedback, and they know you will praise work that is well done. It is important to remove as much of the threat as you can, to create an environment where people feel able to discuss things they could have done better and don't feel penalised for making 'mistakes'.[20] One way to do this is to role-model asking for feedback yourself and show how to use it to further enhance strengths and to shape improvements.[21] Within this environment, you can then approach feedback in a direct and honest way.

The importance of clear feedback is well illustrated in the book *Radical Candour* by Kim Scott.[22] The principle is based on applying the seemingly simple notion of 'care personally and challenge directly'. They draw this as a simple 2 × 2 matrix and contrast it with too much care and not enough challenge (ruinous empathy), too much challenge without sufficient care (obnoxious aggression) or even not enough care or challenge (manipulative insincerity).

Based on our reading, research and experience,[23] here are some suggestions for impactful feedback and feedforward. Rather than producing a generic list of feedback behaviours and mnemonics, we have focused instead on suggestions for some challenging feedback scenarios. These are all based on approaching feedback with care and challenge, by providing specific examples and focusing on the behaviour or outcome rather than the personality or motive (see Table 6.4).

Table 6.4 Feedback and feedforward scenarios

Blind spot	Based on the well-known Johari window,[24] a blind spot is, by definition, unknown to the person you are giving feedback to. Raising awareness of blind spots gives the person the opportunity to change their behaviour, and they will only achieve this through feedback. To help people to reach new insights, encourage them to see the situation from other people's perspectives, putting themselves in the other person's shoes and perhaps suggesting that they seek direct feedback from other people. You can ask questions such as, • *How might this behaviour have come across to other people?* • *How do you think this made them feel?* • *In what ways could this be true?* • *How could you find out more about the impact of this?*
Poor outcome	When there has been a poor outcome, most people will want the opportunity to own up, to admit what went wrong and to suggest what to do differently next time. However, you, as manager, also have some accountability, so turning it into a joint problem-solving session is likely to create a more constructive learning experience than you listing all of the things that you think went wrong. So you could position the feedback in this way: *'We're both disappointed with the outcome. Let's spend some time together to unpick what happened and why. It should be cathartic and will help us both to see what we can learn for next time'.*
Sensitive	Some people really struggle to come to terms with feedback, and they may take time to come to accept and understand it. If you're confident that the feedback is right, then you must stand firm and avoid the temptation to indulge them by backtracking. However, they may need additional support to gain perspective on any negative feedback. This will help them to see it in the context of all of the good things they are doing and clearly signpost some specific actions. Be proactive in reopening discussion on the feedback, with comments and questions such as, *'You seem to be pondering on the feedback. What are you thinking? How are you feeling about it? What are you doing to keep going with all of the good things we discussed? How can I help you to think through the feedback on [specific point]?'*
Broadening horizons	Some people are great performers, but risk being left behind if they don't adapt and develop their skills and knowledge for the future. They need help to be motivated to act now and to be willing to move beyond their comfort zone. This conversation can be introduced as follows: *'Your knowledge and experience of how we do things is incredibly helpful to the team. I'm doing some work looking at how our department will evolve over the next three years. I'd like to work with you to make sure that we build your skills and knowledge so that you can continue to make this contribution as things change'.*
Not hearing praise	Some people carry a lot of self-doubt that makes it difficult for them to hear and accept praise. They are likely to shrug it off and dismiss it as undeserved. Make the praise very specific so it is not discounted as a general comment and flag to the person that you are giving them praise. You may also need to do it in private so it is a pleasurable experience for them rather than embarrassing. For example, you could say, *'I really want to thank you for your contribution to the success of this project. The way you brought in fresh ideas from other businesses really helped unlock our thinking. We wouldn't have got to such a good solution without this input. The results are going to be so much better. It was great work. Thank you'.*

Habit four: looking to the future

Property businesses have a reputation for being cut-throat. Money is often seen as the primary motivator, driving behaviour and making people individualistic, protective of their own deals. This can limit the investment in developing talent. But it doesn't have to be that way. One senior leader we know bucks this trend. He develops his team. He holds a bigger-picture view and has a firm belief that he is responsible for their development. Consequently he involves them in projects, he hands work to them. He looks at a longer-term view of sustainability, thinking how to drive the business forward over the next five years rather than just maximising his personal revenue in the current year. As a result, he has a pipeline of talented people who are taking on greater accountability, helping him to grow faster than others operating in the same market.

If you've worked through the Talent Compass, you will have explored the type of skills and experiences the business requires going forward, based on different business scenarios (your future talent demand). You will also have a sense of the risks associated with this, which things you need for the future may be difficult to find and how you might go about it. In essence, the Talent Compass will help you to shape your team-level talent strategy, identifying scenarios, supply, demand and risk. This can be done as a collaborative activity, leveraging the existing insights of your team and providing them with an opportunity to develop new perspectives, understanding and learning.

However, you also need to factor in your own aspirations. What is your personal vision? How do you want your career to develop? What could get in your way and how? How do you mitigate against that? For example, many highly talented leaders who are ready for a move get 'held back' or 'blocked' from moving because they are seen as too valuable in their current role. In many businesses you can't move internally until there's a viable succession. It is therefore your responsibility to look forward and to ensure that you will be able to move roles without a perceived risk to results.

So part of a 'look to the future' is about mapping the future business needs whilst recognising your own personal needs. As we saw in the Talent Compass, the other stakeholder is the team. Holding a clear focus on future needs is one of the hallmarks of leaders who are exceptional at developing their people.[25] However, according to team members, this is one of the things they find is most often missing in their development conversations, and it's a big frustration. For example, Bart told us, 'I do have some conversations with my line manager about what it could look like for me in the future, but there is very little foresight'. People recognise that you can't make promises or be specific about their career, but they do crave a sense of direction, an understanding of how things could map out. Providing this sense of direction enables people to be proactive about developing their own career and to take action to build appropriate skills, knowledge and experiences, increasing organisational commitment.[26] Conversely, without this support, people often assume that there aren't many future opportunities, and that is when they are likely to start looking for jobs elsewhere. As a leader, you need to get in first. You need to be the one having the headhunter conversation about what the future could look like to facilitate the aligning part of the Talent Compass.

One particular request we often hear is for clearer career pathways, for information showing people how they could progress from their current role, either hierarchically or laterally. Although you may ask them about their future aspirations, many people will say they don't know, and it's often because they need help to understand what some of the options might be. In some organisations, the HR function will invest time in developing possible pathways, but typically these only cover common job categories or families (such as how to become a branch manager in retail or how to become a partner in a professional services firm). Furthermore, with changes in the world of work, they may not be relevant for long. It can therefore be helpful for leaders to invest time in working with the team (individually or collectively) to consider a range of possible routes to develop their careers. There are three common career development routes: within current role, through lateral moves or hierarchically.

The questions in Table 6.5 can help to clarify the options. Preferred scenarios can then be developed and the feasibility of these explored with other

Table 6.5 Looking to the future: questions to identify opportunities

Skills/ knowledge	• What core skills and knowledge does this person/this team have? • Where else might this be valued? • What do these skills/knowledge provide a foundation for developing in the future? (For example, having a core skill in problem solving may provide a foundation for developing project management skills.) • Where else might these skills/knowledge be valued or needed?
Experience/ other attributes	• What experience does this person/team have? • What other attributes do they have? (e.g. relationships or reputation) • Where else might these be valued? (e.g. customer service experience would be valuable in product design to represent the customer perspective.)
Hierarchical progression	• What roles represent the main promotional opportunities for this person or people on this team (within this team or another part of the business)? • What skills, knowledge, experience and other attributes would be needed to be successful in these roles? • How could these be developed?
Lateral progression	• What lateral moves might be of interest to this person/this team (e.g. an opportunity to do more of the work they most enjoy)? • What skills, knowledge, experience and other attributes would be needed to be successful in these roles? • How could these be developed?
Within current role	• What learning opportunities would this person value in their current role? • How would this help them and the business? • How could this be actioned?

stakeholders. Another element of this is the concern of leaders not to raise expectations that can't be delivered. This is important and is part of being transparent and having a trusting relationship. If there are no career development opportunities, it can be valuable to look at adapting the current role to create greater stretch and challenge. This is described in the next chapter from the individual's point of view, called 'job crafting'.

Habit five: working in partnership

In Hays Asia, the leader of one of the best-performing offices of the past five years is very clear on his role. When people first join, he has a conversation with them and explains the way things work. They, he says, are his customer. His role is to give them lots of experiences and support, to help them to be a top performer and to realise their potential. In return, he expects them to be honest about what's working or not working for them and how he can make things work better so they can perform to the best of their ability. His business results are testament to the success of his approach.

The benefits of working in partnership are woven throughout talent liberation, with premise five stating that 'success depends on partnership between the organisation and the people' and 'aligning' being one of the sections of the Talent Compass. Through the previous chapters, we have already explored that partnership is supported through transparency, shared accountability for career development and increasing meaning in work. Within this, the line manager is once again in the front line, acting as a 'broker' to find ways of meeting both individual and organisational needs, alongside their own needs. Many leaders understand that this is their role and get satisfaction from getting it right. However, there are some challenges. For example, the mindset of scarcity can encourage managers to hold on to their talent, prioritising their own short-term needs over the best interests of the individual or the organisation. There can also be a reluctance to engage in career conversations for fear of raising expectations when there are no opportunities to offer. This is difficult. However, avoiding the conversation will not make the issues disappear, and the advice is generally to engage in open dialogue so that you and the team member can reach a conclusion together.

One feature of partnership is that it needs to be genuine. People are more engaged when they feel that their relationship with the organisation really is reciprocal.[27] Within this, the team member needs to feel that you really understand where they are coming from and will seek the best solution for them. In some instances, that may involve the person leaving. If they leave with help and support, following honest dialogue they are likely to be a great ambassador for your business. This helps your employer (and personal) reputation and gives you the opportunity of continuing to network with them and find ways to access their talent in the future if that is appropriate. These and many other advantages of this type of 'giving' are described by Adam Grant in his book *Give and Take*.[28] For example, a focus on what others need (without being concerned that you will get a return) can help you to unlock people's potential, leverage wider networks and create an environment of collaboration. However, this can create a tension between your responsibilities as an advocate for your team and your responsibilities as part of 'management'. Navigating this can be difficult. However, if you are open and transparent with all stakeholders and clear about how information will be shared, then it is possible to be even-handed and to fulfil your responsibilities to your team and your organisation.

Sarah is Head of Group Communications at a global software and services firm. Having recruited a new team member, she became concerned about their performance and engagement, and when they started to take more personal calls at work and book last-minute midweek leave, she became suspicious. So during a weekly check-in, she asked if they were looking for another job, and her fears were confirmed. She explored this further, and they explained that they felt that internal communications were not for them.

Sarah suggested they worked together – with her being flexible and giving them time for interviews (and help in preparing for them) and them working hard at their role and keeping her informed about job offers and a likely leave date.

A few months later, the team member was performing well and told Sarah that they'd decided to stay. In the three years since then, they've gone from strength to strength in their existing role, becoming a top performer. The relationship has remained open and transparent with a high level of trust, respect and loyalty.

From a talent liberation perspective, how can this partnership operate? Table 6.6 is a typical outline, often delivered as a series of conversations, allowing for periods of reflection and information gathering.

Table 6.6 Aligning organisational and individual needs

Explore	Based on 'know your team', explore:
	• What does 'Personal Best' mean in their current role?
	• What Strengths or passions might they want to use more in the future?
	• What do they want to do less of in the future?
	• What type of role, challenges, relationships and work do they want to do?

(Continued)

Table 6.6 (Continued)

Inform	Based on 'look to the future', describe your business needs. Be clear what the opportunities are: • What are the scenarios for how the business might change in the next few years? (e.g. markets, skill requirements, technology, customer needs, etc.) • What are the skills and experiences likely to be most important in the industry/function? • In what ways might this person's skills be developed or deployed in different parts of the business? • How might the current role evolve? • What is your view of their strengths and potential (and the view of other key stakeholders if relevant)?
Plan	Based on the insights from 'explore and inform': • Where is the common ground? • What are the differences in wants and needs? • What options are there for meeting as many of both parties needs as possible? • How could we move this agenda forward? • How can we track our progress and continue to check that it's meeting our combined needs?
Connect	Based on the plan, broaden the network of people invested in this: • Who else can support us in achieving this (e.g. leaders in other areas, the people team, external networks, etc.)? • How can we engage them in the process?

Reflections

Christie is an ambitious and entrepreneurial small business owner. She employs ten people, and talent liberation is key to her business model. She operates in a competitive market, where repeat business is essential for survival. The market can be quite fickle, so it is vital to build your reputation and to always deliver customer service excellence. Christie is very careful about whom she recruits. She wants people with the same drive and passion that she has. She wants people who are committed to technical excellence and are always keen to learn, to do more and to be the best they can be. She recruits people who show this, and then she nurtures it in them. She genuinely cares about her team and invests in them. She allocates some of her time to training them. She pays for external courses and encourages people to learn new techniques. She provides opportunities for them to learn from each other and to be constantly improving. Christie has a compelling vision for the future, one that includes her team, providing opportunities for them to be their best and to explore their passion. As a result, the business is booming. Whereas competitors are often plagued by turnover of their experienced staff, people stay with Christie. She brings out the best in them.

Overall our message is clear. To drive business success, leaders must be actively developing their people to perform at their best in their current role and to prepare them for what might be next. This may not be captured as a formal objective. It may not be measured, but it isn't an optional extra. This is the job of every leader in every business[29] every day, not just when there's a box to be filled in on the appraisal form!

In this chapter we have described five habits of leaders as liberators: knowing your team, being a catalyst for growth, feeding back and feeding forward, looking to the future and working in partnership. There is a logic to the way we've described them. It is probably easiest to start with 'know your team' and then to progress from there, but we think it is possible to start somewhere else or in several places at the same time. If you develop these habits, you create opportunities to liberate the talent of those around you. These habits will help you to liberate your own talent too as you will be able to take a step up instead of constantly feeling the pull of being down in the detail. If you don't develop these habits, your talented people may stagnate, they may not be able to keep up with any changes, they may do the bare minimum, or they may vote with their feet and leave. Yes, if you do these things, they may still leave, but if they do, they will leave as a strong performer and someone who will be an advocate for you and your business.

- Who would refer to you as a liberator of their talent?
- How well do you know your team, their attributes, aspirations and frustrations? How could you get to know them more?
- How often are you a catalyst for growth, providing learning and development opportunities for your team? How could you do this more often?
- How could you encourage your team to take accountability to create their own learning opportunities?
- How can you apply some of these habits to be a catalyst for your own learning?
- How strong are you at giving feedback and feedforward?
- Do your team recognise feedback when you give it?
- How much do you look to the future and think about future opportunities for your team? How clear are they?
- How well do you manage to work in partnership with your team and find common ground between what they want and what the organisation needs?
- What will you do differently as a result of reading this chapter?

Notes

1 For more on these definitions of talent, please refer back to chapter one.
2 'In at the deep end' experiences or highly challenging assignments have been shown to have a positive impact on job performance and career development, particularly in early

career. For example, see Carette, B., Anseel, F. and Lievens, F., 2013. Does career timing of challenging job assignments influence the relationship with in-role job performance? *Journal of Vocational Behavior* 83(1), 61–67.

3 For example, Wendy Axelrod, David Clutterbuck, Marc Effron, Roland Smith, Michael Campbell, Karen Kram, Wendy Hirsh, Jane Yarnall, and Sarah Bosley. Specific references are also given where relevant.

4 *The 7 Habits of Highly Effective People* has been a highly influential book since its publication in 1989. Covey, S., 1989. *The seven habits of highly successful people.* London: Fireside/Simon & Schuster.

5 For examples of the business benefits of engagement, see Gallop and Aon Hewitt annual surveys. Further benefits are also given in the Centre for Evidence Based Management, www.cebma.org/wp-content/uploads/Evidence-Based-Practice-The-Basic-Principles-vs-Dec-2015.pdf (accessed 22.03.2019). The personal benefits are supported in other research. For example, see Axelrod and Coyle, 2011, Axelrod, W. and Coyle, J., 2011. *Make talent your business: How exceptional managers develop people while getting results.* San Francisco: Berrett-Koehler Publishers.

6 This is a common theme in our qualitative and quantitative research within organisations. Team members often express frustration that their managers do not invest enough time in supporting their learning and development. See also Smith, R. and Campbell, M., 2011. *Talent conversations: What they are, why they're crucial and how to do them right*, 1st ed. Greensboro, NC: Centre for Creative Leadership.

7 The full report can be found at www.cipd.co.uk/Images/employee-outlook_2017-spring_tcm18-21163.pdf. The response rate for the percentage of line managers who discuss training and development needs has been adjusted to correct for the 11 percent of respondents who indicated that this question was not applicable to them (accessed 22.03.2019).

8 LinkedIn learning report can be found at https://learning.linkedin.com/resources/workplace-learning-report-2018 (accessed 10.05.2019).

9 See an article on the accountability ladder at www.talentstrategygroup.com/application/third_party/ckfinder/userfiles/files/The%20Accountability%20Ladder(1).pdf (accessed 14.05.2019).

10 For an introduction to unconscious bias and how to identify and overcome it, visit the resources of the Employers Network for Equality and Inclusion at www.enei.org.uk/diversity-inclusion/unconscious-bias/ (accessed 01.07.2019).

11 Talent spotter is a leadership role suggested by Hirsh, W., 2015. *The role of the line in talent management.* London: Institute for Employment Studies. Talent Scout is suggested by Marc Effron at www.talentstrategygroup.com/application/third_party/ckfinder/userfiles/files/The%20Talent6%20Model-%20Growing%20Talent%20Faster.pdf (accessed 01.07.2019).

12 John, working with colleague Laurie Cohen: Arnold, J. and Cohen, L., 2008. 1 the psychology of careers in industrial and organizational settings: A critical but appreciative analysis. *International Review of Industrial and Organizational Psychology* 23, 1–44.

13 This was originally positioned in 1996 as the way people are most likely to learn and address their development needs. Lombardo, M. M. and Eichinger, R. W., 1996. The career architect development planner, 1st ed. Minneapolis: Lominger. It has since gained considerable popularity as a way to think about learning, but there is little evidence to support it.

14 This was originally referred to as the 'Eisenhower matrix', as it was used by Dwight D. Eisenhower, thirty-fourth president of the United States from 1953 until 1961. It was later popularised by Stephen Covey in his book, *The 7 Habits of Highly Effective People* (see endnote 5) and his later book, *First Things First.* Covey, S. R., Merrill, A. R. and Merrill, R. R., 1995. *First things first.* London: Simon and Schuster.

15 Developed in the 1980s and 1990s, this was popularised by Sire John Whitmore (among others). Whitmore's influential book, *Coaching for Performance: The Principles and Practice*

of Coaching and Leadership, has a special twenty-fifth anniversary edition, published by Nicholas Brealey Publishing in 2017.

16 The idea of 'Nudge' has been popularised, for example, through the influential book on the topic: Leonard, T.C., 2008. Thaler, R.H. and Sunstein, C.R., 2008. *Nudge: Improving decisions about health, wealth, and happiness.* New Haven, CT: Yale University Press.

17 https://ceo.usc.edu/files/2018/07/Performance-Feedback-Culture-Drives-Business-Performance-i4cp-CEO-002.pdf (accessed 26.03.2019).

18 Research indicates that our unconscious biases may influence the type of feedback we give to different people. This can disadvantage some groups. For example, it has been suggested that women may be given less direct and challenging feedback, thereby limiting their opportunities to grow and develop. Correll, S. and Simard, C., 2016. Vague feedback is holding women back. *Harvard Business Review,* https://hbr.org/2016/04/research-vague-feedback-is-holding-women-back (accessed 16.09.2019).

19 For an engaging (and short) introduction, see Carol Dweck's TED talk: www.ted.com/talks/carol_dweck_the_power_of_believing_that_you_can_improve#t-608499 (accessed 20.03.2019). However, it is noted that there are some challenges to the growth mindset approach. For example, see https://aeon.co/essays/schools-love-the-idea-of-a-growth-mindset-but-does-it-work (accessed 20.03.2019).

20 For more information on this, see the work on trust, cooperation and a circle of safety by Simon Sinek. For example, www.bing.com/videos/search?q=Simon+sinek+safe+youtu be&&view=detail&mid=E9724A59F07BF1CD67F2E9724A59F07BF1CD67F2&&FOR M=VRDGAR (accessed 01.07.2019).

21 For example, see Steelman, L. A. and Wolfeld, L., 2018. The manager as coach: The role of feedback orientation. *Journal of Business and Psychology* 33(1), 41–53.

22 For some helpful tools and more information on the book, visit the website www.radical candor.com/ (accessed 26.03.2019).

23 This has been assimilated over a number of years, and we are therefore unable to provide specific additional references.

24 Developed by Joseph Luften and Harry Ingham in the 1950s and widely used in personal development and training. For a simple introduction, see www.communication theory.org/the-johari-window-model/ (accessed 26.03.2019).

25 This was one of the findings in research by Axelrod and Coyle, 2011. *ibid.*

26 Moon, J. S. and Choi, S. B., 2017. The impact of career management on organizational commitment and the mediating role of subjective career success: The case of Korean R&D employees. *Journal of Career Development* 44(3), 191–208.

27 2017 Trends in Global Employee Engagement: https://insights.humancapital.aon.com/talent-rewards-and-performance/trends-in-global-employee-engagement-2017?utm_source=ceros&utm_term=engagement17 (accessed 20.03.2019).

28 Published in 2013 by Weidenfeld and Nicolson. For more information and a summary, visit the Give and Take website, www.adamgrant.net/give-and-take (accessed 26.03.2019).

29 Involvement of line managers in the talent agenda has been shown to be strongly correlated with business success. For example, see Cantrell, S. and Benton, J.M., 2007. The five essential practices of a talent multiplier. *Business Strategy Series* 8(5), 358–364. And the growing trend to hold leaders accountable for developing talent, www.talentstrategygroup.com/application/third_party/ckfinder/userfiles/files/Top%205%20 Management%20Trends%20for%202018(1).pdf (accessed 20.03.2019).

7   Liberating your own talent

Introduction

We have seen how HR professionals, leaders and line managers can create an environment that is conducive to talent liberation, but how can you be proactive and liberate your own talent? How can you find ways to use all of your skills and experiences in a way that you find motivating and enjoyable? How can you continue to grow and develop? Referring back to the talent quadrant from Chapter 1, how can you use your natural Strengths and work towards being at your Personal Best? If you believe that you are High Potential, how can you develop this potential and achieve your ambitions? This chapter explores these questions, providing practical tools to help you to liberate your own talent. We first draw on the concept of 'thriving at work', which we introduced in Chapter 2. We then explore four scenarios that we often encounter:

- I want to liberate more of my talent now.
- I want to see how I can develop and use more of my talent in the future.
- I work on a series of short-term assignments, but I want to take a long-term view of my talent
- I have a lot of talent, I am ambitious, and I want to progress as a High Potential.

For each scenario, we offer practical tools and activities based on our coaching and consulting work. We also draw on research across academic literature (such as the career literature, counselling, mentoring and coaching).[1] In doing this, we consider personal strengths, skills, experiences, aspirations and some of the psychological factors that may influence us such as beliefs, mindset or confidence.[2] There are many personal benefits to be gained from spending time reflecting and planning on how you use and develop your talent at work. For example, building and using career development skills has been associated with many increased career success, career satisfaction, perceived employability and better work-life balance.[3]

Within this chapter, we refer to career as well as to talent. We see career as an ongoing relationship between you and your work. Career is not a single decision about vocation. Rather it is how you use and apply your talent at work throughout your working life. Career management and planning are the reflections, insights and actions you can take to have greater fulfilment, which includes how your talent can be liberated. This fulfilment can arise from goal-focused action to achieve a specific ambition over a number of years (such as building the skills, qualifications and knowledge to be a doctor, engineer, mechanic or pilot). It can also be fulfilment from being the best you can be at your work, be that serving customers, managing your team or offering financial advice. Liberating your talent can involve following a dream, but it also captures how you respond to emerging opportunities that you don't have control over.[4] With the increasing pace of change and workforce uncertainty, there is a growing recognition of the importance of career management skills. Indeed with the workplace changes described in Chapter 2, new work opportunities are likely to continue to evolve. Fewer people are likely to engage in an organisational career throughout their working life. Rather you may experience periods of traditional employment, periods of working independently, time working in small niche providers and time reskilling. Thus, the ability to be proactive and to manage these transitions becomes an important life skill. Previous chapters have described some of the ways in which organisations can help people to build these skills (for example, educating people on career development). Governments are also aware of the need to build these skills across the workforce. For example, a recent research project involving eight European countries was tasked with developing free access tools to support with career self-management.[5]

Thriving at work

> When people describe what they want from work, it can often be summed up by the term 'thriving'. For example, Jane, an experienced manager, told us, *'I'm not hugely ambitious. I like a challenge, and I want to thrive, but I don't want to be on the succession plan'*.
>
> Others tell us of wanting to *'recognise that I'm adding value'* or to have *'ongoing stimulus, challenge and enjoyment, wanting to feel that I've learnt something every day and that I've managed to do something I thought I couldn't'*.

As described in Chapter 2, the idea of thriving at work has gained considerable attention across academic, policy and practitioner literature.[6] When someone is thriving, they can be seen to be growing and learning, making a contribution and feeling energetic and enthusiastic about it. Thriving is a state where talent is freed and people are able to work at (or towards) their Personal Best. It is focused on our relationship with work rather than any external measure of achievement. The academic literature has helped to define thriving at work and to develop ways of measuring it. The typical definition shows a person combining vitality (energy and enthusiasm for work) and learning (building and applying knowledge and skills).[7]

We have found it helpful to represent thriving at work as a simple diagram which positions thriving as high learning and high vitality, but also illustrates the alternative energy if either learning or vitality (or both) are missing (see Figure 7.1). For example, if you are being stretched and challenged but do not feel energised, there is a risk of burnout, or 'stressing'. If you are engaged and energised but do not have a great deal of stretch or your skills are not being fully utilised, then you may feel that you are 'stalling'. You have more to offer, but no way of using it. Finally, without energy, engagement or learning, you are likely to be 'withdrawing', doing the bare minimum and seeing work as 'just a job' rather than a place for your talent to be used to the benefit of you and your organisation.

At times, however, you may make an active choice to be somewhere other than 'thriving'. For example, in later career or during times of change or caring responsibilities, there may be a conscious decision to be in 'stalling'. In these situations, people describe their relationship with work as 'maintaining', they are happy with their role and recognise that they do not want to invest the resources

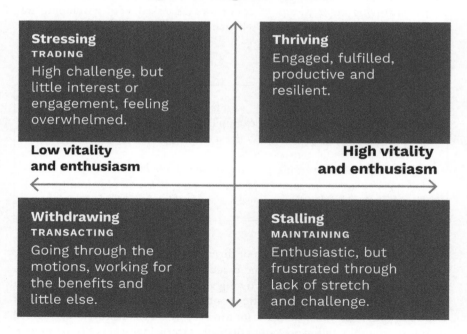

High learning and stretch

Stressing
TRADING
High challenge, but little interest or engagement, feeling overwhelmed.

Thriving
Engaged, fulfilled, productive and resilient.

Low vitality and enthusiasm

High vitality and enthusiasm

Withdrawing
TRANSACTING
Going through the motions, working for the benefits and little else.

Stalling
MAINTAINING
Enthusiastic, but frustrated through lack of stretch and challenge.

Low learning and stretch

Figure 7.1 Thriving matrix

or time in moving to thriving. At other times, you may have your sights set on a longer-term goal and accept that you will spend some time first in 'stressing'. For example, accountancy trainees put up with boring work and challenging exams in order to qualify and access more interesting future opportunities. This is a type of 'trading', accepting that there is a longer term pay-off, and such delayed gratification is a good predictor of career success as measured by salary and promotions.[8] Equally, there may be times when we take on work that we don't really want because we simply need to earn some money and we are involved in 'transacting' (offering our time in return for cash).

Thriving at work has been associated with many benefits to the individual (as well as to the organisation). For example, some of the individual benefits when thriving at work include:[9] sustainable high performance, psychological well-being and a sense of meaningfulness through work. For us, the language of thriving at work captures the essence of talent liberation from the individual's perspective. Our goal is therefore to help more people to reach a place where they are thriving at work, which brings clear benefits to them personally, as well as bringing benefits to their organisation through increased performance and engagement.

Some people would seem to have more of a predisposition to thrive at work than others. For example, relating thriving to personality and the 'big 5' factors,[10] people who are high on extraversion and conscientiousness but low on neuroticism are more likely to report thriving at work. Similarly, people who see themselves as worthy and competent and hold positive beliefs about their ability to take control are more likely to report that they are thriving at work.[11] However, this does not mean that people with different traits or self-beliefs cannot also thrive. We hope that the rest of this chapter will help to show how this can be achieved.

- Where are you on the thriving matrix?
- Can you think of times when you were in each of the other quadrants?
- What was happening, and how did it feel?
- Right now, where would you like to be on the thriving matrix?
- Looking to the future, where would you like to be on the thriving matrix?

Liberating my talent now

Marco was frustrated. He'd recently got a new manager who didn't seem to understand what he was capable of. His previous line manager had trusted him and got him involved in lots of complex projects. However, now he was back doing just the simple projects. To make it worse, he also had to check with his manager before making any decisions. He felt that he'd taken a step backwards, and he wasn't happy.

Petra had been doing the same job for five years. Some things had changed, but it was basically the same role. She was getting bored. She could see lots of opportunities to improve processes and provide better customer service. She knew that she had so much more to offer, but no one seemed to see it.

Wanting to liberate more of your talent now is often associated with finding ways of moving into 'thriving' from one of the other sections on the thriving matrix. To make this change, it is helpful to start with some diagnosis, developing insights into your current talents and your current situation to enable you to identify what action you can take.

Developing insights

Developing insights about your talent is a bit like being a detective. You're looking for clues, following lots of different lines of enquiry and getting input from a range of witnesses. You are never sure which bit of information will lead to a breakthrough, so you need to keep an open mind and not close things down too quickly, even if they don't seem to be leading anywhere. An 'incident room' (see Figure 7.2) can give you a visual record of all of your data, stimulating you to see new connections and to reach new insights about yourself and your context.

Figure 7.2 The incident room

There are lots of questions and activities that you can do to prompt you to develop these insights (see Table 7.1). You will be able to answer some of these questions by yourself. For others, you will need to seek input from others – the witnesses who can give you their feedback, perspective and thoughts.[12] One key witness is likely to be your line manager, and this is one of the important ways in which team member and line manager can engage in conversations that help both parties and create an environment for matching organisational need and individual aspirations (see Chapter 6 for more information). More information on each part of the incident room can be found in section E in the Tools and Resources at the end of the book.

Taking action

Having developed some insights, you can think about changes you want to make that can quickly move things towards thriving. We have supported people taking a range of steps depending on their situation and aspirations. The following examples are intended to illustrate some common actions rather than be an exhaustive list. Some of these will be completely within your control. Others will require you to work with other people (such as your line manager) to agree to some specific changes. Given the influence of the line manager, we include one action on how to engage them in your desire to liberate more of your talent.

Table 7.1 Developing personal insights

My story so far	• A timeline of your life and career, including significant events and how you felt about them
My strengths and weaknesses	• A summary of your key strengths and weaknesses, including your skills, knowledge, experience and behaviours, plus anything that you can see holds you back
My values and interests	• The main things that interest and motivate you and the values you live by
My adaptability	• Your approach to learning, change and taking control, along with the extent to which you value and seek change or predictability
My view of careers	• Your personal theory of career[13] and what you think helps people to get on, what holds them back and how you make career decisions
My current organisation	• Your organisation's needs and the extent to which there seems to be 'alignment' and 'fit'[14] with what you can want and what you can offer[15]
My careerscape[16]	• The nature of opportunities available to you in your current line of work
Reflections	• What have you found out about yourself? • When are you most likely to thrive? • What is missing at the moment that means you are not thriving?

- *Setting a short-term goal.* You've captured how things are at the moment through the incident room. What is that you want to change? How do you want things to be different in the near future? Where do you want to be on the thriving matrix, and how will you know that you are there? For example, in the previous scenario, Marco might want to be empowered to run complex projects. Petra might want to instigate and lead a process improvement.

- *Growing your talent.* You may identify that you are missing a specific skill, experience or behaviour. Think how you can fill this gap and who can help you. Online resources or books can provide excellent guidance, as can informal conversations. You may also look for support from a coach or attend a training programme. You need to be willing to try out some different things and take some risks. It's then helpful to cement your learning by asking three key questions: what went well, what didn't go well and what will I do differently next time. Petra may identify that she needs to build her influencing skills to help her to put forward her suggestions.

- *Crafting your role.* There may be more scope for adapting your current role than you realise. The term 'job crafting' refers to the proactive ways in which you can adapt your role to make it more fulfilling for you personally, often without the involvement or knowledge of your manager.[17] This challenges the traditional idea of job design as something done from the top down, but is seen to bring benefits to the organisation as well as to the individual. In the previous example, Marco has previously done some job crafting to broaden his remit to more complex projects. His frustration is now that he is back to doing the basic role.

- *Challenging unhelpful beliefs.* Many people subconsciously hold themselves back from being their Personal Best. We have encountered many leaders who hold a belief that they need to know everything that is going on. This keeps them in the detail, preventing them from spending time on the added value activities that they are meant to be doing. Their behaviour is unlikely to change until they challenge this underlying belief. This isn't easy, but by identifying current beliefs and why you might hold on to these, it is possible to challenge assumptions and build new, more helpful beliefs that can help you to thrive.[18] For Petra, a belief that 'my views aren't worth listening to' could be holding her back.

- *Looking after yourself.* To be able to perform at your best and to thrive at work, you need to look after yourself, particularly when you identify that energy is low. There are many books and articles that encourage you to improve your well-being. The key behaviours of eating, sleeping, relaxing and exercising have been described by Dr Rangan Chatterjee as 'The Four Pillar Plan[19]. His approach provides the science behind these habits and offers practical ways for you to build them into your daily life.

- *Engaging your line manager.* Many people feel that their line manager is holding them back and stifling their talent. To address this, we suggest that you start by putting yourself in their shoes. What are they trying to achieve, what really matters to them and what are they worried about? Understanding their agenda, hopes and fears can help you to think how you can find common ground and match their needs with yours. Conversations are the best way to do this, and you may need to invest time in building trust before you can give them open feedback on how you feel and what you want to change. The sections on feedback and feedforward in Chapter 6 can help with this. In the previous example, this is likely to be a key focus for Marco.

Whatever action you choose, you will be taking greater accountability to shape and control your work. This in itself is likely to lead to greater support from your organisation as part of what is called 'social exchange theory'.[20] Having identified some short-term actions, it is important to continue to review your progress and to see this as an ongoing process of self-awareness, reflection and planning. For example, Richard told us about his approach.

'Every 6–12 months, I reflect on my career and think where I am going. I draw a circle and mark how happy I am with different parts of my life and think, *What am I going to do about it?* I also think, *What do I like?* I think it's really important that your job is something you like; otherwise it has an impact on other things in your circle. I also think, *What am I good at? What market value does this have?* I do the preparation on my own, and then I go and talk to some other people about it – five or six people whom I really trust and will give me a different perspective. These people are trusted friends and confidants. This then helps me to decide on any changes I want to make'.

- What insights have emerged?
- What immediate actions will you take?
- What else do you plan to do?
- Who can help or support you?
- What could get in your way, and how can you manage this?
- How will you review and measure your progress?

Setting a future direction

Becky was looking for a career change. She'd had enough of working in sales and wanted something completely different. She knew that she had lots of transferable skills, but she didn't know what she wanted to do or how to go about it.

> Paul was looking to progress his career. He wasn't really ambitious, but he didn't want to stay where he was forever. He wanted to get a sense of his options and to feel that he was working towards something that he would continue to enjoy and find rewarding.

Many people don't know how they want their work to develop or how they want their talent to be used in the future.[21] This accounts for the internal cringing that people can feel when asked the classic appraisal or interview question, 'Where do you see yourself in five years'? However, the absence of a specific career goal does not mean that you won't benefit from a plan. Indeed, if your plan is simply focused on a very specific goal or destination, this can lead to real difficulties once this is achieved.[22]

As with liberating more of your talent now, we see that setting a future direction has two elements, developing insights and taking action.

Developing insights

You may be reluctant to set yourself future work goals, especially if you don't have a particular ambition. However, extensive evidence from motivation and goal theory indicates that setting a goal and direction is an important way to motivate ourselves to act. This direction may be a specific career goal or job, such as to be a partner in a firm or to set up your own business. It may also be more generic, such as using particular skills (e.g. leading a marketing campaign) or making a particular contribution (e.g. supporting students to get into university). To develop insights about your future career direction, it helps to take different perspectives. We suggest three in particular: dreaming, balancing and evolving. Each of these can lead to a different set of options, which can then be brought together into thriving or liberation goals in a 'connecting' phase (see Figure 7.3). In addition to these, it can be helpful to collect some psychometric

Figure 7.3 Three perspectives on future direction

data on careers that may suit your personality and interests. One example of these is the Self-Directed Search (SDS), based on John Holland's vocational personality theory.[23] In the previous examples, both Becky and Paul are likely to benefit from starting with a broad review of their work and career. This can then inform the action they choose to take.

- Dreaming. *'I want to find a way to combine my passion for the outdoors with my paid work'.*
  This can be really helpful in getting you in touch with your passions, switching off the realistic and critical side of your brain that may stamp on new ideas before they've been developed.[24] The idea is to enter a world where anything is possible and there are no barriers to you doing what you'd love to do. To get in touch with your dreamer ideas, it can be helpful to apply creativity techniques such as visualisation, drawing or playing games of 'what if' (asking questions such as 'What if I didn't have to earn money'? or 'What if I could live anywhere'?). Once you've done your dreaming, you can bring back the rational and critical side of you to explore your dream in more detail. For example, you could think realistically and explore what skills, knowledge, experiences and resources you would need to acquire to make your dream come true. Your critic may challenge if you really would like this role, and that can prompt you to find a way of testing it out. Where possible, it helps to invest time in getting some hands-on experience and meeting people who are already doing the role you aspire to. A number of organisations can assist you with this, making appropriate introductions to support career transitions.[25] These activities can help you to make an informed choice rather than making a change that you later regret. You can also use your dream as a starting point to explore how you could move towards it. What goal could you choose that would take you closer to your dream? Dreaming may be particularly valuable to Becky as she considers her overall career direction.
- Balancing. *'The most important thing is that my work is local so I can be there for my kids. But I also want to keep learning and feel that I'm making a valuable contribution'.*
  Because it is important that your work goals are considered within the context of other things in your life, you may consciously choose not to 'thrive' at work. Many people therefore complete a version of a 'life-wheel' activity. Typically, this involves drawing a circle and segmenting it into eight segments, each with a label (such as work, finance, health, family, friends, leisure, learning, spiritual and community). A time scale is then chosen (for example three years), and a goal for each segment is written, followed by a 'current score' showing how close to the goal you currently feel. The interaction between different elements can then be reviewed to expose synergies and apparent contradictions. (For example, if a work goal is 'work two days per week' and a finance goal is 'save for a house deposit', it would seem that these goals are difficult to achieve simultaneously, and one may need to be

prioritised.) A template and instructions for the life wheel can be found in section F of the Tools and Resources.

- Evolving. *'I love my role, and I don't want to change it. However, I'd really like to get a bit closer to the customers so I can see the impact of what we're doing and offer better service'*.

  It may be that you're quite content with your current working life. In which case, your goals are likely to be focused on small changes, to keep your energy, interest and learning as well as maintain your relevance to the organisation by adapting and building appropriate skills. One way of thinking about this is using 'traffic lights'. Red: What am I doing now that I want to *stop* doing? Amber: What do I want to *change* and do more of or less of? Green: what do I want to *start* doing? Answering these questions may lead to goals about building particular skills, working on particular projects or taking on additional accountabilities. These may be working gradually towards new roles, promotions or specialisms, but it's likely to be a more gradual change than that suggested by the 'dreamer'. However, as the word 'evolving' denotes, you should expect this to continue changing so it will be important to continue to revisit your goals. In the previous examples, Paul is likely to benefit from particular attention to evolving.

Having explored your options through the lenses of dreaming, balancing and evolving, it is time to do some connecting. Making connections is about trying to synthesise the data that you've collected, identifying the direction you want to move in to liberate more of your talent or to move closer to thriving. You may choose to do this via an extension to your incident room, looking at the themes that emerge and mapping your different options. Because it's a creative process, it can be difficult to predict what will emerge, and it may take some time to develop clarity.

Taking action

As your picture for the future emerges, you can start to consider the action you want to take (if any). As previously, the examples given here are intended to illustrate some possible activities that might be involved. For our mini case studies, Becky and Paul, they might both need to take action in all or some of these areas. You may also need to challenge your preconceived ideas of what is possible and be creative in finding solutions. For example, one entrepreneur we have worked with relocates every six months. He has found a way to combine his passion for his business with his passion for travel. Last heard, he was in Bali.

- *Collecting experiences.* Consider what experiences you will need to be credible in the type of work you want to do. To do this, you may need input from people doing the role or people who recruit/commission them. Understanding what these experiences are is particularly important if you are keen to move into a new area of work. Similarly, if you want to progress into management and leadership roles, flatter structures create fewer opportunities to gradually take on management responsibilities, so you need to be proactive in developing relevant experiences. These experiences can be gained through project work, secondments or voluntary work. For example, running a fundraising charity event or coordinating the work of a group of volunteers would provide credible experience of management and leadership.

- *Developing new skills and qualifications.* Some future roles will require very specific skills or qualifications. Again, it is helpful to get advice on what these are and the options for how you can get them. This can sometimes be a long-term commitment. For example, if you want to retrain as a psychologist or as a teacher, it may involve several years study, and you may need to be creative about how to balance your dreams with your other commitments and needs. You may also need to develop new skills and behaviours. For example, if you aspire to move into a senior leadership role, you will need to learn to get things done through others, avoiding the temptation of being overly involved in the details.

- *Continuing your professional development.* Continued professional development (CPD) is essential for safeguarding your employability in your existing line of work.[26] Furthermore, the ability to keep learning and to be 'learning agile' has been cited as one of the most important skills for the future.[27] As seen in the thriving matrix, learning it is also fundamental to thriving at work. There is widespread agreement that anyone can develop or increase their learning agility across the four areas of mental agility, people agility, change agility and results agility?[28] If you want to build your learning agility, there are three simple habits. First, be a conscious learner by using the three questions we introduced earlier as part of growing your talent (what went well, what didn't go well and what I will do differently next time). Second, broaden your perspective. Avoid the temptation of quickly jumping to a conclusion, and instead be curious. Always ask yourself, 'How else could I tackle this? Who else has tackled similar issues? How can I find out about different solutions? Third, actively engage in a range of learning and development activities to develop skills and knowledge. A list of possible continuing professional development activities is included in section G in the Tools and Resources at the end of the book.

- *Building networks.* Research suggests that the majority of new roles are secured as a result of networking rather than roles being advertised.[29] Your network can also provide invaluable sources of feedback, information and opportunities for building your experiences and learning. A strong network will include team members, managers, peers, leaders in other functions and people outside your current organisation. In terms of career, five particular 'career shaper' roles have been identified.[30] An Advisor can offer opinions and suggestions for how to develop your work in a particular direction. An Informant can offer knowledge about particular work and what is required. A Witness (as discussed previously) can give you feedback on your strengths and weaknesses. A Gatekeeper has the power to provide access to roles, opportunities or resources. An Intermediary can positively influence or advocate on your behalf. It can be helpful to map your current network and see if you have people who are fulfilling each of the shaper roles and identifying how to fill any gaps. Remember that networks tend to function on the basis of 'reciprocity', so be clear what you can offer people in your network.[31]

- What are your future goals?
- What are the things that you need to do to achieve these goals?
- When could you do each of these things?
- What could get in your way, and how will you manage this?
- What help or support do you need?
- How will you review and measure your progress?

Thriving as a contingent worker

Simon had worked as a contractor since being made redundant eight years earlier. He had spent most of the time working on a range of projects for one client. In the early days, he found the work highly challenging, stimulating and rewarding. He was thriving. However, as time went on, he found the projects straightforward. He knew he was adding value to his client, but he was not enthused by the work. He knew he was stalling.

Julia worked as an interim HR director. She found the start of each assignment stressful. She was in overload as she worked to get to grips with the strategy, culture and politics of each new organisation. She felt that projects always ended just as she had built her understanding of the business. She was therefore constantly feeling overwhelmed and was never able to capitalise on her learning.

As we have seen, changes in the world of work mean that more people are likely to be working independently at some point in their career. Independent working is likely to involve some variation of working as a 'freelancer', contracting for specific projects within your field of expertise. This work may be secured directly with the client or through a broker (such as those described in Chapter 2). Equally, the work may involve working with the same people for a sustained period (as for Simon), or it may be a series of shorter assignments (as experienced by Julia). Each situation will be different, but each will bring challenges for thriving at work. We have identified three core challenges to thriving as a contingent worker:

- *Ready now.* When organisations outsource work to an external person, they expect someone who already has the required skills, knowledge and experience. Consequently, there is typically little appetite to invest money or time in training or developing these people.
- *No active engagement.* As previously discussed, although freelance workers may be strategically critical, they are not employed by the organisation. Consequently there is little attention paid to their engagement or to activities to help them to keep high vitality and enthusiasm.
- *Transacting.* When working independently, there is no guarantee of income. Consequently decisions to take a particular role or assignment can be driven by economic necessity for the money rather than an interest in the work.

Thus, if you are working independently, it may be difficult to find a role where you can thrive. You may instead find yourself in a negative space, perhaps stalling (like Simon) or stressing (like Julia). You may also at times decide that you are happy to be maintaining, trading or transacting. However, if you do want to thrive, you will need to be proactive in shaping your work opportunities in both the short and long term.

Developing insights

Work on employability is particularly helpful for exploring the situation faced by contingent workers. The aim is to secure the job you want whilst also being ready for the next role.[32] Many of the activities already described in this chapter are very helpful for developing insight on your current situation (the incident room) and on your aspirations for the future. However, the section on 'my careerscape' (the opportunities available to you) and your future direction are likely to be more complex. The following questions will help you to explore these in more detail. They are drawn from models of marketing and business strategy.[33]

- *What market am I in?* Understanding your current market and how it operates is important if you want to be proactive and to exercise control over the type of work you are doing. Points to consider include: who are my clients? What do they need from me? What is my relationship with my clients? Who are my competitors? Who are the potential new entrants to this market? What substitutes could my clients use? How might this market change or evolve in the next few years? What are the risks I need to manage?
- *What market do I want to be in?* These questions relate to the dreaming, evolving and balancing insights in the previous section. This is where you reflect about your current work and think about the environment and the type of work you want to be engaged in. This may involve more of the same, or you could look to work with new clients in new markets or to

extend the range of services you offer. You may want to move to thriving, but you may decide that at the moment you are happy to be somewhere else on the thriving matrix. You may also decide to capitalise on the flexibility offered as a contingent worker and consciously take on some roles just for the economic value whilst other roles are taken on for fulfilment. Referring back to our earlier examples, both Simon and Julia would benefit from considering the market they want to be in and therefore any changes they want to make.

- *Why me?* This question is about your unique selling point and why your clients will choose you. Do you offer something that is different to others in the market? Do you offer it at lower cost? Do you have specialist industry knowledge? Are you offering a particular professional or technical skill? Alternatively, your offer may be about your relationships or the way you carry out your work.

Having considered these questions, you can reflect on your situation and the options open to you.

Taking action

As a contingent worker, you need to take accountability to stay ahead of the game. If you don't, there is a risk that your skills and services could become obsolete, or you could end up doing the same thing time and again with little stretch and challenge. It is therefore essential to continually invest in the four activities described previously for setting a future direction (collecting experiences, developing new skills and qualifications, continuing professional development, building networks). Investing in these can be particularly difficult for contingent workers, with economic consequences from any cost of training plus loss of earnings through investing time in learning rather than working. It is therefore important to be clear on the motivation to take action. There are a number of potential sources of motivation (such as meaning, building competence, enabling future progress and social interaction).[34] It is helpful to understand what your motivation is so you can focus on the personal benefits and gains from engaging in ongoing learning. Some contingent workers also spend time in networking groups or with a personal coach to encourage them to take action to safeguard future employability as a contingent worker and to help them to thrive in their work.

- Which part of the thriving matrix am I currently in?
- What market am I in?
- What market do I want to be in?
- How could I enter this market, and who could help me?
- What action will I take to transition to where I want to be?

Developing my high potential

Sally had always been identified as someone with 'High Potential'. It had given her lots of opportunities, and she knew she'd progressed faster than lots of other people. But now it felt as if she'd reached a plateau. No one was showing her the next steps, but she was ambitious and still wanted to move up the ladder.

Amir saw himself as a late developer. He had not taken a traditional route in his career, but he had gradually progressed. However, over the past 12 months, he'd become aware that he had a lot to offer. He was bright and technically strong. He had good people skills, and he realised that he was also now really motivated to progress. But his manager saw him as a safe pair of hands rather than as someone with potential.

If you have the ability and motivation to be in the top 15–20% or performers in your particular field or profession, then you can be considered to fit the High Potential description in our talent quadrants (from Chapter 1). In order to develop your potential, it will be helpful to engage in all of the activities described in the previous sections (building insights, taking action to liberate your talent now and having a sense of future direction). These actions will help you to build the skills, experiences, behaviours and networks and so on that will help your success. However, if you are within the High Potential quadrant, there are some additional things to consider. To do this, we are using emergence and effectiveness as two key characteristics of High Potentials.[35] People with High Potential need to invest time in building both.

Effectiveness and emergence

People who are strong at effectiveness are good at delivering the results. They can be relied upon to make things happen, to build a team, to develop innovative solutions and to consistently perform. If you have High Potential, you need to make sure that you are effective. If for some reason you cannot perform or deliver, you need to do some problem solving to resolve this.

One characteristic of people who are highly effective is that they often invest their time in doing the job and can miss out on the importance of making sure that other people recognise the contribution they are making. In other words, they can neglect the activities of emergence. Without investment in emergence, your potential is unlikely to be noticed, which will limit the opportunities you are given, which in turn will limit your ability to further grow and develop your talent. In our earlier example, Amir would appear to be high on effectiveness but is perhaps neglecting to pay attention to emergence.

In contrast to effectiveness, people who are strong at emergence are likely to be good at being noticed. They are likely to have a strong network and be adept at making sure that their achievements are well known. Often active on social media and visible to those with power, they are likely to cultivate their reputation and personal brand. This may involve steps such as developing a clear identity, managing perceptions and taking action to match intended identity with the impressions of the intended audience.[36] However, too much time invested in these activities can be associated with a number of career derailers, including exhibitionism and arrogance.[37] Within the context of talent and career, emergence is likely to involve talking with people about your aspirations and engaging them in helping you to put your plans into action. In our earlier examples, it is likely that Sally needs to invest time in understanding why her progression seems to have slowed. She probably needs to ensure that she is delivering on effectiveness and then to ensure she engages with people who can help her to continue to develop her career.

In order to develop your potential, it is helpful to reflect on your current effectiveness and emergence, taking account of your own perceptions but also seeking input from others (see Table 7.2). Having done this, you can identify any actions you need to take.

Table 7.2 Effectiveness and emergence: audit and actions

Current effectiveness	*Actions to increase effectiveness*
• How well do you currently deliver in your role? • What data do you have on your current effectiveness? (e.g. targets, team engagement, and formal assessments) • How do others describe your ability to deliver? • How do you make sure that you balance all of the demands of your role?	• What gets in the way of your effectiveness? • What could you do about this? (For example, could you build your own skills, increase skill or engagement in your team, seek additional resources, find new approaches or renegotiate expectation?) • What support and help do you need to increase your effectiveness?
Current emergence	*Actions to increase emergence*
• What is your current reputation? • What do you want to be known for, and how do you manage your reputation? • Who knows about your current and past achievements? • Who knows about your strengths, aspirations and hopes for the future? • Who do you use to help you in your current role and to help you to develop for the future?	• Think about how you want to be seen by others, and identify what you can do to fill any gaps between how you are seen and how you want to be seen. • Broaden your network (see previous section) and engage in conversations with people about what you want and how they can help you. • Identify any beliefs that may hold you back from engaging in emergence (see previous section).

Reflections

This chapter has emphasised the importance of you taking accountability for liberating your own talent and taking action to enable you to thrive at work (if that is what you want). Using four scenarios (liberating my talent now, setting a future direction, thriving as a contingent worker and developing my High Potential), we have introduced many practical tools that you can use to help you to liberate your own talent. These tools, approaches and activities can also be used to help others, to open up new conversations and to encourage those around you to be proactive in liberating their talent too.

Ongoing learning and continued professional development are the primary themes of this chapter. Indeed, given workplace changes, the only way to safeguard your employability is through ongoing investment in the knowledge, skills and experiences you can offer. You need to be entrepreneurial. You need to think about future market needs and your own interests. You need to use these insights in order to continue to grow and develop yourself as someone with relevant skills, someone whom people want to work with. In many ways you need to think of yourself as a 'product' with a market, competitors and unique selling points. Like any product, you also have a variety of routes to market, and different routes may be appropriate at different times. You no longer need to feel constrained by only considering permanent employed roles. Instead you have countless options of flexible working within one organisation or across several organisations. You may work independently or collaborate with others in similar roles. You may be fortunate enough to work from a location of your choice or to intersperse periods of work with periods of travel, artistic endeavours, retraining or voluntary work. However, to take advantage of these opportunities, to liberate all of your talent, you need to be proactive. As someone told us recently in an interview, 'It's your career, your life. If you don't make it happen, no one else will'.

- How close are you to thriving in your work at the moment?
- What are your short- and long-term career aims?
- Why are these important to you?
- How will you feel when you achieve these aims?
- What action can you take to move towards these?
- What help and support do you need?
- What could get in the way, and how will you overcome it?
- How can you continue to reflect and act on your career?

Notes

1 For example, Greenhaus, J. H., Callanan, G. A. and Godshalk, V. M., 2009. *Career management*. Thousand Oaks, CA: Sage; Hirsch, W., 2007. Career development in employing organisations: Practices and challenges from a UK perspective. *Career Research & Development*, p. 18; Egan, G., 2013. *The skilled helper: A problem-management and*

opportunity-development approach to helping. Cengage Learning; Allen, T.D. and Eby, L.T. eds., 2011. *The Blackwell handbook of mentoring: A multiple perspectives approach.* Chichester: John Wiley & Sons.

2 These have been referred to as the 'Cognitive-Affective Personality System'. See Heslin, P. A., Keating, L. A. and Minbashian, A., 2018. How situational cues and mindset dynamics shape personality effects on career outcomes. *Journal of Management*, 0149206318755302.

3 Research suggests those with clear career goals tend to experience higher subjective and objective career success. For example, see Akkermans, J. and Tims, M., 2017. Crafting your career: How career competencies relate to career success via job crafting. *Applied Psychology* 66(1), 168–195.

4 For example, see Krumboltz, J. D., 2009. The happenstance learning theory. *Journal of Career Assessment* 17(2), 135–154.

5 ACUMEN project, based on the Career Management Skills Framework for Scotland (2012).

6 For example, the academic work of Spreitzer and colleagues (e.g. Spreitzer, G., Porath, C. L. and Gibson, C. B., 2012. Toward human sustainability: How to enable more thriving at work. *Organizational Dynamics* 41(2), 155–162) and the policy work of the UK government on mental health at work (e.g. https://assets.publishing.service.gov.uk/government/uploads/system/uploads/attachment_data/file/658145/thriving-at-work-stevenson-farmer-review.pdf) and the research of Mercer (e.g. www.mercer.com/our-thinking/thrive/thriving-in-a-disrupted-world.html).

7 Spreitzer, G., Sutcliffe, K., Dutton, J., Sonenshein, S. and Grant, A. M., 2005. A socially embedded model of thriving at work. *Organization Science* 16(5), 537–549.

8 Converse, P. D., Piccone, K. A. and Tocci, M. C., 2014. Childhood self-control, adolescent behavior, and career success. *Personality and Individual Differences* 59, 65–70.

9 These examples are drawn from a range of articles, including Spreitzer, Porath, and Gibson, 2012; Taneva, S. K. and Arnold, J., 2017. Thriving, surviving and performing in late career: A mixed-method study of pathways to successful aging in organizations. *Work, Aging and Retirement* 4(2), 189–212; Walumbwa, F. O., Muchiri, M. K., Misati, E., Wu, C. and Meiliani, M., 2018. Inspired to perform: A multilevel investigation of antecedents and consequences of thriving at work. *Journal of Organizational Behavior* 39(3), 249–261.

10 Personality is generally considered to have five key traits: Openness, Conscientiousness, Extraversion, Agreeableness and Neuroticism.

11 This has been termed the 'core self-evaluation'. For more information, see the Walumbwa article cited above (endnote 10).

12 Different people are likely to shape our career in different ways. 'Witness' was a term used to describe people who can give a fresh perspective. For more information on this and the other categories, see Bosley, S. L., Arnold, J. and Cohen, L., 2009. How other people shape our careers: A typology drawn from career narratives. *Human Relations* 62(10), 1487–1520.

13 This has been termed our 'career worldview'. See Bosley, Arnold and Cohen, 2009 as referenced above.

14 There has been considerable research on person-organisation fit. This seems to suggest that a high perceived 'fit' is associated with higher performance, organisational commitment and positive organisational citizenship behaviours. For example, see Boon, C., Den Hartog, D.N., Boselie, P. and Paauwe, J., 2011. The relationship between perceptions of HR practices and employee outcomes: Examining the role of person – organisation and person – job fit. *The International Journal of Human Resource Management* 22(1), 138–162.

15 For a model of employability, looking at the internal and external labour markets and how this relates to personal and occupational attributes, see Rothwell, A. and Arnold, J., 2007. Self-perceived employability: Development and validation of a scale. *Personnel Review* 36(1), 23–41.

16 The term 'careerscape' is used in Inkson, K., Dries, N. and Arnold, J., 2014. *Understanding careers: Metaphors of working lives.* London: Sage, 294.

17 For more information, see Tims, M. and Bakker, A. B., 2010. Job crafting: Towards a new model of individual job redesign. *SA Journal of Industrial Psychology* 36(2), 1–9.

18 For more information, see the work of Kegan and Lahey on YouTube and also their book, Kegan, R. and Lahey, L. L., 2009. *Immunity to change: How to overcome it and unlock potential in yourself and your organization*. Boston: Harvard Business Press.

19 For more information on the 'four pillar plan', visit https://drchatterjee.com/about/ (accessed 16.04.2019).

20 For example, see De Vos, A., Dewettinck, K. and Buyens, D., 2009. The professional career on the right track: A study on the interaction between career self-management and organizational career management in explaining employee outcomes. *European Journal of Work and Organizational Psychology* 18(1), 55–80.

21 When asked this question in workshops, typically only one in ten has a clear direction, although in some industries and professions (such as banking and accountancy), there appears to be much greater clarity.

22 For example, Ed Catmull (founder of Pixar) recounts his sense of feeling lost once his life's goal of releasing a first feature-length film (*Toy Story*) had been achieved. For more of his story, see Catmull, E. and Wallace, A., 2014. *Creativity Inc: Overcoming the unforeseen forces that stand in the way of true inspiration*. London: Bantam Press.

23 The SDS can be completed for a small fee. Visit www.self-directed-search.com/ for more information (accessed 03.07.2019).

24 The 'rational, dreamer, critic' model is widely associated with the work of Disney. It was brought to the fore by Robert Dilts, e.g. Dilts, R., Epstein, T. and Dilts, R. W., 1991. *Tools for dreamers: Strategies for creativity and the structure of innovation*. Cuperinto, CA: Meta Publications. For a helpful summary, see also Barton, M., Müllerova, J. and Svobodova, I., 2012. Disney strategy in management-inspiration from arts and creative industries. https://appsconf.files.wordpress.com/2016/01/2012.pdf (accessed 20.08.2019).

25 Young people are encouraged to find out about career options and to work-shadow to gain more information. As you get older, this becomes more difficult, but it remains an important part of making career decisions. To address this gap, a number of innovative organisations are providing services to help adults explore career options. For example, see www.vive.work/.

26 CPD is also associated with other benefits, including increased confidence, self-efficacy and resilience. For example, see Mackay, M., 2017. Professional development seen as employment capital. *Professional Development in Education* 43(1), 140–155.

27 For example, see the interviews conducted by McKinsey, www.mckinsey.com/featured-insights/future-of-work/the-digital-future-of-work-what-skills-will-be-needed.

28 There are different models of learning agility. The information presented here is based on the Lominger model (see https://bettsolutions.com/wp-content/uploads/2014/04/Learning_Agility_-_De_Meuse_Dai_Hallenbeck_2010_.pdf for more info). Also helpful is the approach taken by the Centre for Creative Leadership (see www.ccl.org/wp-content/uploads/2015/04/LearningAgility.pdf).

29 For example, see a LinkedIn survey that suggests that as many as 85 percent roles are filled through networking, www.linkedin.com/pulse/new-survey-reveals-85-all-jobs-filled-via-networking-lou-adler/ (accessed 16.04.2019).

30 See Bosley et al., 2009 as referenced in endnote 13 above.

31 This is based on social exchange theory Blau, P. M., 1968. Social exchange. *International Encyclopedia of the Social Sciences* 7, 452–457.

32 Herbert, I. P. and Rothwell, A. T., 4–6 January 2016. *Employability and contingent finance professionals in the knowledge-based economy*. Singapore: Chinese and American Scholars Association.

33 For example, commonly used tools such as Porter's five forces, Ansoff's box, nine specimen strategies and product life cycle. For a summary of these and other management models, including full references, we recommend Harding, S., 2017. *MBA management models*. London: Routledge.

34 Herbert and Rothwell, 2016.
35 We have taken these labels from work by Hogan Assessments. To download a report explaining these, visit www.hoganassessments.com/thought-leadership/the-politics-of-potential/ (accessed 03.07.2019).
36 For example, see Khedher, M., 2015. A brand for everyone: Guidelines for personal brand managing. *Journal of Global Business Issues* 9(1).
37 This is well described by the 'Hogan Dark Side', where too much of a positive trait can lead to unhelpful behaviours. Hogan, R. and Hogan, J., 2001. Assessing leadership: A view from the dark side. *International Journal of Selection and Assessment* 9(1–2), 40–51.

Part III – Appendix

Toolkit and resources

This section provides additional detail and examples of some of the ideas introduced in earlier chapters. Having taken advice from practitioners about what would be most helpful, we have included the following:

A   A full set of Talent Compass questions, with examples (providing you with more detailed questions to guide you, building on the questions introduced in Chapter 4);

B   A Talent Compass solution guide with example risks and actions that other organisations have taken. This includes further sample processes, ways of engaging across the talent ecosystem and how to promote a more positive talent climate (from Chapter 5). Whilst mostly drawing on our work with organisations, some of the examples also cite additional research;

C   Further questions to explore when to 'borrow, buy or build' talented people (from Chapter 5);

D   Examples of everyday learning opportunities to support leaders in habit two, catalyst for growth (from Chapter 6);

E   Further questions to support a personal 'incident room' (from Chapter 7);

F   Life wheel activity to explore goals (from Chapter 7); and

G   Questions to explore options for continued professional development.

A   Full set of Talent Compass questions

This section provides a full set of questions to accompany the Talent Compass. We suggest that they are used to frame your conversations, helping you to view each part of the Talent Compass from a range of perspectives. It is also helpful to seek input from a range of people, particularly for the sections on aligning, formal process and informal talent climate. We have found that these questions can be answered very differently by different groups of internal stakeholders.

---

1   What are your key strategic aims?

We understand our organisational priorities, strategy and values.

Questions:

- What are your key strategic aims? (e.g. what markets do you serve? In what way do you serve? And how do you want to differentiate on value, service or innovation?)
- What do you see as your organisational strengths, weaknesses, opportunities and threats (e.g. your reputation, your employment brand, new market entrants, or tack of innovation)?
- What values and practices shape the way your organisation operates (e.g. level of openness, compliance with process, or devolved decision making)?
- What are the possible scenarios for how your organisation may evolve and grow (e.g. new markets, products, services, or technology)?
- What are the organisational priorities and risks that the talent strategy needs to address (e.g. diversification of product services, scalability to maintain reputation and agility during growth)?

2   Short-term talent supply

We know what talent we have easy access to and have identified short-term talent risks.

Questions:

- Which are the strategically most important skills, knowledge, experience and roles that the organisation should have access to for the short term (e.g. senior populations, key roles, customer excellence, operational or financial management, new markets)?
- What is your visibility of the current supply of people with these skills/in these roles (e.g. assessment of their skills, potential and performance, length of time in role, length of time to become competent in the role or potentially hidden sources)?
- What do you know of the current levels of motivation and engagement of people with these skills/in these roles and more widely across the organisation (e.g. survey data, attrition rates, Glassdoor rating, sickness absence rates, indication of how much people are working 'at their Personal Best' and what type of 'High Potential' you have)?
- What partners do you currently work with to help you to find the skills and experiences you need in the short term (e.g. recruitment agencies, contracting agencies, crowd sourcing sites or outsourcing)?
- What difficulties have you encountered in the past 12 months in finding people with the skills, experience and knowledge that you need (e.g. time to recruit, fit between what was wanted and what was available or length of time for people to become productive)?
- Which other organisations are looking for people with these skills, knowledge and experience (e.g. what opportunities you need to compete with)?
- What changes do you anticipate to this supply in the short term (e.g. new sources of internal or external supply, new threats from competitors opening nearby or change in the economic situation)?
- What are the risks that emerge from reviewing these questions (e.g. cost of oversupply of skills that aren't needed, scarcity of required skills and experiences, high attrition, lack of visibility or limited network of partners)?

3 Future talent demand

We understand our likely future talent needs and have identified long-term risks.

Questions:

- Which individuals or groups of people are critical to deliver your long-term strategic objectives (e.g. the roles and people that you see as driving your long-term competitive advantage or success)?
- What are the key talent implications for each scenario explored as part of your organisational goals (e.g. new language or technology skills, knowledge of mergers and acquisitions or understanding of regulatory requirements in new markets)?
- What else could influence your future talent needs (e.g. the possible impacts of changes in technology, demographics or internal and external structure on your future talent needs)?
- What is the role of disruptive talent for your future success (e.g. the people who will 'shake things up' and bring fresh perspectives)?
- What are the key gaps between what you have now and what you need in the future (e.g. gaps in leadership skills, diversity, numbers of people with specific skills or experiences, number of people operating at their 'Personal Best' or pipeline of 'High Potential')?
- How confident are you that any talent gaps can be filled (e.g. internally or externally)?
- Which of these future talent need gaps do you think you can fill internally, and what actions would you need to take to achieve this (e.g. need for more project managers, action would be to identify people who are interested and have potential to take on this role, provide training to agreed standard or explore how the work of those moving into this area can be backfilled)?
- What are the risks that emerge from reviewing these questions (e.g. likely scarcity of a specific essential skill suggesting a need to review the strategy or look at operating in a different geography, cost of specific skills or lack of visibility of the talent ecosystem)?
- Which of these future talent needs will you look to fill externally through external hires, contractors, hired experts or outsourcing, and what actions would you need to take to achieve this (e.g. specific skills, projects or tasks and the partnerships needed to fill these gaps)?

4   Aligning

We work in partnership with our people to align the organisation's wants and needs with the individual's wants and needs.

Questions:

- How clear are you on the wants and needs of the different groups of people you work with? (e.g. on a scale of 1–10 for different employee segments, how well do you understand their motivations, interests, aspirations, hopes and fears?)
- How clear are they on the needs and wants of the organisation? (e.g. how well do they understand your short- and long-term needs for skills, knowledge and experience, the critical roles and the risks you observe?)
- How do you create a shared understanding and alignment of wants and needs? (e.g. what is the forum for this and the opportunities for people to develop and grow in their preferred direction?)
- How transparent and supported is the 'career deal'? (e.g. how clearly do people know how to get on round here? How do they get feedback on their strengths? How well are they supported to self-manage their career?)
- How do you support achievement of wider life goals (e.g. connecting work to a wider sense of meaning and work-life balance or supporting flexibility, outside interests and corporate social responsibility activities)?
- How do you assess the attractiveness of the work offer including financial, benefits, developmental opportunities and other factors relevant to the individual (e.g. comparison with your competition and other opportunities open to an individual, perceived fairness, location, benefits package, status or acceptance rate of new recruits)?
- What is the individual's responsibility in finding alignment? (e.g. how are they encouraged to take accountability for aligning their needs with the organisation's needs?)
- What are the risks that emerge from reviewing these questions? (e.g. lack of clear career deal makes it difficult to attract and retain, along with lack of interest in aligning organisational and individual needs, lack of support for career self-management or negative impact on engagement.)

5   Informal talent climate

Our climate helps everyone to perform at their best in the interests of achieving goals.

Questions:

- How well do you utilise the skills, knowledge and experiences of your people? (e.g. how well deployed are people? How well empowered are they, especially those who are in strategically critical roles? How well are they supported and encouraged to be at their 'Personal Best' and to develop their potential?)
- How well do you engage and support disruptive talent? (e.g. are they encouraged and listened to, or do they find themselves isolated?)
- How are managers encouraged and supported to focus on the development of their people? (e.g. is there recognition for managers who export talent to other parts of the organisation? Is there recognition for managers who meet the individual needs of team members?)
- In what ways is people's learning and agility valued and rewarded? (e.g. is a sideways move for learning purposes celebrated as much as a promotion? Are there positive stories about learning, career and risk taking? Is learning shared across boundaries in collaborative and open ways?)
- What is your appetite for risk in people decisions? (e.g. are you willing to move an internal candidate into a role early to avoid looking externally?)
- How diverse is your organisation? (e.g. are people from diverse backgrounds attracted to work with you and encouraged to stay? Does your organisational diversity reflect the diversity of our customers?)
- How open and honest are people? (e.g. does the climate support open conversations and direct feedback, or do people generally keep quiet? Is information about succession and talent openly shared?)
- How do things change when under pressure? (e.g. are these behaviours/approaches core to the organisation or just seen as a 'nice to have'?)
- What are the risks that emerge from reviewing these questions (e.g. the informal talent climate that doesn't support learning, growth or engagement)?

6   Formal processes

Our formal processes help the organisation and our people to meet their short- and long-term goals.

Questions:

- What formal talent processes do you use (e.g. assessment, succession, development planning or on-boarding)?
- What is the purpose of these, and what value does each add to the organisation (e.g. succession purpose to manage key person risk, impact monitored through six-monthly updates on succession and all key roles having at least one identified successor)?
- How transparent are the formal processes, and how are they perceived by the stakeholders who the processes are about? (e.g. development plans are openly shared, and individuals feel supported, encouraged and enabled to act on them.)
- What are the unintended consequences of the processes (e.g. assessment of potential not being shared with individuals driving a culture of secrecy)?
- How engaged are senior leaders in the talent processes (e.g. driving the process, fully engaged and participating, compliant or actively disruptive)?
- What structured support do you have to encourage learning and knowledge sharing (e.g. formal training programmes, job rotation, digital learning platforms or learning sets)?
- How do you encourage internal applicants for roles (e.g. visibility of opportunities, guaranteed interviews or feedback session for all internal applicants)?
- What flexibility do you offer to encourage people to work with you in a variety of ways (e.g. contract working, home-based opportunities, annual hours or part-time roles throughout the organisation)?
- What information is there to help people to map their career (e.g. providing accessible information on career pathways, sharing examples of how people have developed their own career or communicating easy routes for gaining additional experience)?
- What are the risks that emerge from reviewing these questions (e.g. gaps in what the processes are delivering in terms of shared learning and career development opportunities or lack of clear added value from some existing processes)?

7 Plan

We have a plan to manage our talent risks and to help individuals and the organisation to achieve their goals.

Questions:

- What themes emerge from the whole Talent Compass (e.g. over-reliance on external hires or lack of encouragement for leaders and managers to grow talent)?
- How do different parts of the system interact? (e.g. is there a recurrent theme or something that seems to be causing other problems?)
- What are you already doing well? (e.g. maintaining and building on the things that are already working well can lead to some high-impact quick wins.)
- What further data do you need to collect to help you to understand risk (e.g. requests of recruitment partners to build greater visibility of talent availability)?
- Which are the biggest short- and long-term talent risks to address (e.g. long-term risk of lack of disruptive talent to develop innovative solutions to future challenges)?
- How can you leverage aligning informal talent climate and formal processes to address these risks (e.g. training and supporting individuals to be more active in managing their own career)?
- How and when will you review the compass and keep it live (e.g. take action and review in six months)?
- Who are the stakeholders for addressing these risks, and how will you involve them (e.g. the CEO, external investors, people in the High Potential category or people with scarce skills)?
- What short-term actions can you take to address the key risks and how (e.g. set up knowledge transfer sessions or a structured onboarding programme)?
- What longer-term actions can you take to address these key risks (e.g. clarify long-term talent needs, develop partnerships with agencies who can source talented people or set up flexible working options)?

B   Talent Compass sample solution guide

For the purposes of this table, we have identified risks and example actions for each element of the Talent Compass. However, we recognise that the talent risks may be collated as themes and that action in one element of the Talent Compass will impact others (in keeping with our systems view). For example, introducing flexible contracts to support future talent demand is likely to have a positive impact on aligning. These examples are intended to help you to develop your thinking on what could work in your own situation.

What are your key strategic aims?	
We understand our organisational priorities, strategy and values	
Sample risk	**Sample action**
Lack of clarity of possible scenarios and talent implications	Discussion with senior stakeholders to explore these in more detail. The questions in the Talent Compass can help to guide this conversation.
Need to prioritise agility as a key strategic talent goal	Work with the senior stakeholders to review the organisation structure and processes for the future – challenging which roles/skills need to be employed and which can be sourced in alternative ways (see section C on when to 'borrow, buy or build').

Short-term talent supply	
We know what talent we have easy access to and have identified short-term talent risks	
Sample risk	**Sample action**
Lack of visibility of people with the required skills, experiences etc. who are available now for key roles	Utilise existing systems to capture people's skills, experiences and aspirations in a way that can easily be searched to find a match. If this is a key risk, explore options for a system that is designed to give visibility of talent.
Lack of availability of people with the required skills, experiences etc. who are available now	Review which skills you are missing and consider alternative ways to access these (e.g. to borrow or buy – see later section). Build relationships with partners so you understand more about what skills are available. Develop contingency plans. For example, recruit people with some of the basic skills and develop fast-track training to develop the required capability.

Not attracting the talented people to work with us	Identify what would attract people to work with you (whether as buy, build or borrow). Explore why they are not being attracted. (e.g. is it poor communication of the offer, or is there a material difficulty such as location? Does the competition offer something more attractive?) Develop and test possible solutions.
Talented people don't stay, creating additional gaps in supply	Conduct research to try to understand why these people are leaving. Identify if there are different categories or segments with different needs (e.g. certain professions, age groups or locations). Work with groups of talented people to understand what needs to change in order for them to want to stay. Develop plans and action as appropriate, for example, job enrichment or further development opportunities. Ensure the research covers people who are employed as well as people working with the organisation in other ways (see also aligning).

Future talent demand

We understand our likely future talent needs and have identified long term risks

Sample risk	Sample action
We don't understand what skills and experiences we need for the future	Work with stakeholders to map future requirements. Seek additional input from industry thinkers (e.g. to recognise the value of disruptive talent). Test thinking and explore how to embed throughout the people processes (e.g. recruitment, development, assessment of potential or reward).
We anticipate finding it hard to find people with the right skills and experiences to meet our needs	Reflect on where you are looking for talented people. Identify opportunities to access more talented people by broadening diversity and inclusion. This could be done by actively seeking people who are looking for career change or people who are leaving military service. More flexible employment contracts may also attract new sources of talent and enable people to work with you from different geographies.
We require unique skills and knowledge which are very difficult to find	Invest in a long-term training and development programme to build the skills and knowledge you need and to build in any likely attrition. Ensure you work in partnership so these people feel valued and want to stay. Also build contingency plans for how you would adapt if these unique knowledge and skills were no longer available.

Aligning

We work in partnership with our people to align the organisation's wants and needs with the individual's wants and needs

Sample risk	Sample action
Lack of visibility of internal opportunities makes it difficult for people to understand the opportunities available to them	Encourage movement of people through always advertising vacancies internally. Review how well internal advertising of vacancies are working and explore how they can be improved, using insights from the world of internal communications.[1] Track the number of internal moves as an important measure of internal mobility.
Individuals expect to be told their next career move and are reluctant to take accountability	Help people to understand how they can manage their own career, clearly stating expectations, describing the 'career deal' and helping people to develop 'career competencies'.[2] Involving people in designing the materials can increase uptake. Training internal coaches and mentors can provide additional support, giving people a sounding board to help them to proactively manage their own career.
Lack of employee engagement and poor rating of the employee experience	Set up two-way communication channels so you find out what your team really thinks and involve them in developing solutions. Give each team leader a simple way of showing appreciation and thanking people for their contribution. Create opportunities for people to build relationships across different teams, for example by 'show and tell' or 'lunch and learn' sessions. Include non-employed people as well as those directly employed.

Informal Talent Climate

Our climate helps everyone to perform at their best in the interests of achieving the organisation's goals

Sample risk	Sample action
People see learning as something that only happens on formal training courses	Share stories and examples of how people learn on the job, making it simple and accessible. Help people to set up informal learning networks to share resources and talk about their learning, linking it to proactive career development (see aligning).
People don't value sideways moves and see upwards as the only way to develop their career	Communicate and celebrate cross-functional and sideways moves, challenging assumptions that careers are only developed through vertical progression. Share stories and examples to illustrate how sideways moves can build skills, aid cross business collaboration and support career development.

Leaders want to recruit people who are 'ready now' and have all of the skills and experiences for a role rather than people who are 'ready soon' and can quickly grow into the role	Instigate conversations on recruitment risks so that leaders factor in the full risks of external recruitment rather than just focusing on the risk of not having specific skills and experiences. For example, explore the risk of fit, length of time to make a contribution, unknown weaknesses, retention risk of internal candidates who are 'ready soon', retention risk of new hire if they are completely 'ready now' and therefore have few growth opportunities and cultural implications of high numbers of external hires.
Leaders don't prioritise developing their teams	Support managers to have better conversations about learning every day. Use examples in Chapter 6 to help leaders see how they can develop their team at the same time as delivering results. Encourage senior leaders to ask their direct reports about how they are developing their teams. Recognise those who are great at developing their team.

Formal processes	
Our formal processes help the organisation and our people to meet their short- and long-term goals	
Sample risk	**Sample action**
We don't know how to assess people's leadership potential	Research has identified a number of measurable traits for leadership potential, for example, ambition, ability, agility and achievement.[3] These can be accessed through a combination of psychometrics (ability, motivation and personality), 360-degree feedback, performance reviews and structured interviews. These should be consistently applied to ensure fairness. The approach should also be reviewed to check the validity of the approach being taken.
We are not leveraging the benefits of diversity in our approach to talent	Collect data on current diversity and explore why some groups may not be attracted, developed or retained. Pilot and test actions to address some of the perceived barriers. Provide training to leaders on self-awareness to help them to be aware of (and therefore to challenge) their biases.
We don't develop our High Potential people to meet our future needs	Review your approach to developing your High Potentials. Map each person's current skills and experiences against your strategic scenarios and your future talent demands. Identify the perceived gaps in abilities, mindset and experiences. Involve the High Potentials in the process so they can shape an appropriate development programme and take ownership for it. Tailor development to the individual and the group, with personalised coaching and mentoring as well as group development and experiences.

We need to capture and share knowledge	Identify where your biggest risks are (e.g. high number of expected retirees or retention issues in a particular function). Work with stakeholders to pilot and test knowledge transfer approaches such as changes in job design, job rotations, secondments, networking events or collaboration on shared projects. Consider developing a database of who knows what (linked to current talent supply).

Plan

We have a plan to manage our talent risks and to help individuals and the organisation to achieve their goals

Sample risk	Sample action
There are not enough resources to support the talent agenda	Most strategies involve compromise and prioritisation. Consider what resources you can get and explore how to invest them for maximum impact. There is a lot that can be done informally. For example, you can create a group of 'early adopters' and people who share your talent vision. These people will role-model and talk about what they do, encouraging others to follow.[4]
There is a lack of board engagement in talent	The risk approach outlined in the Talent Compass can engage senior leaders in the talent agenda in new ways. If they seem unwilling to engage in the Talent Compass conversations, you can identify some appropriate actions, start small, conduct some pilots and demonstrate the benefits. This will give you data to make a case for their involvement and additional resources.

C   When to borrow, buy or build

The different ways of accessing talent were introduced in Chapter 5. The following table provides additional information to help you to consider when to apply which approach.

Type of talent	Best suited when . . .
Internal existing talent (deploy now or develop for the future)	• Context is unique, so the person can perform their role better if they are part of the organisational system and understand how to get things done and are able to role-model the values. • The contribution of these tasks/or this role is strategically important. • The requirements are likely to be medium or long term. • There is no particular cost benefit in using a different employment model. • The required skills are available, and people with those skills are interested in being employed *Example: appointing an internal candidate to an Operations Director role*
Partnership	• Requirement may be short term or sporadic, requiring a specialist skill or experience set (which could be strategic), such as implementation of a new system or development of a new brand strategy. • Requirement may be a long term, but non-core activity, such as outsourced service desk or security services. • A partner is available who can service your needs in a more cost-effective way than you could internally. • The scale of the work makes it inappropriate for a single freelancer. *Example: Procter & Gamble's Connect + Develop; contracting with a consultancy to deliver a particular project or outsourcing set tasks to another organisation*

(Continued)

Type of talent	Best suited when . . .
Freelance	• The worker can do their work better based on understanding the context for the work and building relationships with the organisation. • The work may be a clearly defined short-term project or a longer-term arrangement based on delivery of agreed pieces of work. • Either the worker or the organisation wants the flexibility of easily stopping the work. *Example: retaining services of legal support or engaging a freelance consultant to run leadership training*
Crowdsourced	• Work can be readily broken into smaller, easily explained tasks that can be conducted remotely. • Little background knowledge is required on the task or the organisation. *Example: data collection, graphic design or innovation challenges*
Co-opetition	• Competitors share a similar challenge and see the opportunity to collaborate to reach a lower-cost or stronger solution than they could on their own. • Trusting relationships exist to support the success of the work. *Examples: collaborations on design and sourcing between car manufactures or joint ventures to create scale to meet the needs of large-scale projects or to lobby government*

D   Examples of everyday learning opportunities

Habit two of leaders as liberators is 'catalyst for growth'. This describes the importance of building learning into everyday activities. Here are more details and examples to help you to integrate these into your work.

Projects	Projects provide an important opportunity for new learning experiences and stretch beyond the normal day job. Things to consider are:

- How can you set the project up to maximise learning (e.g. roles, scope or visibility of project)?
- What added value projects could you instigate as learning opportunities (e.g. improving an existing process, conducting some research with internal/external customers or exploring competitor offering)?
- How can you create opportunities for your team to support projects in other areas of the business?

Team meetings	Typical team meetings may be transactional and focused on business updates and short-term problem solving, not longer-term issues. However, team meetings can become a critical source of learning. We've seen leaders do this through:

- Allocating the first 10 minutes of the meeting for someone to share an article or piece of news relating to their market or sector. (This can rotate round so everyone takes a turn.)
- Giving more detail on how decisions have been made so people understand more about the context, the options and the thinking process which led to the decision, including how to engage stakeholders and support implementation.
- Sharing accountability for chairing the meeting and producing the actions.
- Using a checklist of questions to support team decision making. (e.g. what are the benefits of this decision? What are the downsides? What is the impact on the customer? What are the alternatives? What could go wrong? How do we make sure this is successful?)

One to one updates or check-ins	Most leaders meet with their direct reports at least monthly. This is an important time to work through some of the 'Know your team' questions outlined earlier. You can also use it to follow up on any development actions you have agreed, making sure that they are still on the agenda, rather than waiting until the annual review. The questions you ask can also help people to reflect on their learning, making it a more conscious approach. Helpful questions include:

- What are you really pleased that you've achieved over the past month? How can you repeat this?
- What has been particularly challenging or difficult? What have you learned from this?
- What do you want to achieve in the next month? What help do you need?
- What different behaviour could you try out as an experiment and then review how it went?

Coaching	Coaching is recognised as a key development tool, and many leaders will be informally or formally coaching their team. To make the most of this, it is helpful to link it to specific development goals. The well-known GROW acronym[5] is a helpful way to structure your coaching.

- GOAL: what problem are you trying to solve? What does success look like?
- REALITY: what is going on at the moment? What have you already tried? What do you think the key issue is?
- OPTIONS: how could you solve this? How else? And if you had limited time, what would you do?
- WRAP UP: which option will you go with? How can you make this happen? When shall we revisit this?

Big bets	People will only get their 'in at the deep end' experiences if someone will take a bet on them. This involves being willing to put them into a role a bit early or to give them a very stretching project. There is some risk in doing this, but also risk in not doing it.

- How can you give this person an 'in at the deep end' experience to fuel their learning and development?
- What are the risks and how can these be minimised (whilst not detracting from the experience)?

Nudge	Nudge[6] is an approach to influencing behaviour through positive reinforcement and triggers, making it more likely that people will choose the desired option. Widely used in politics and public health, it can also be applied to encourage ongoing learning. For example:

- Make it easy for people to make choices that support their learning. An example is showing that learning is a simple activity supported by asking three questions every day: what went well, what didn't go so well, and what will I do differently next time?
- Make it visible, share what others are doing to develop themselves, role-model, and talk about what you are doing. This will encourage others to do the same.
- Motivate and remind by sending out nudge emails and reminders on development actions[7] so people can track their progress and deliver on their intentions.
- Make it part of a 'learning regime'[8] where learning is an explicit outcome that is monitored and reviewed, with rewards for following the process and negative consequences for noncompliance.

E   Completing your personal incident room

To liberate your talent, you need to develop insights about yourself and your work environment. The following table provides more detail and examples on the headings of the 'personal incident room'.

My story so far	People often link their story to a timeline, a visual CV which captures significant events of education, work, influences and feelings. The thriving matrix can provide a way to capture how you felt about your work at key points. You can then explore what was it about these times that contributed to you thriving (or wherever you were on the diagram). It can also be interesting to consider key influences throughout your story so far. Who or what has influenced you to make particular decisions?
My strengths and weaknesses	This is a favourite question at interview or in appraisal – typically being met with a very 'safe' answer which has very little insight. However, to liberate your talent, it is important to develop self-awareness. What are your current strengths and weaknesses, including your skills, knowledge, experience, behaviours and anything that you can see holding you back? The widely drawn 'Johari window'[9] provides a helpful way to broaden your self-awareness. The 'public arena' (known to self and others) will be easy for you to identify, and if you spend time reflecting, you will be able to list the strengths and weaknesses of your 'private self' (known to you but not to others). It can help to look through lists of qualities rather than starting with a blank sheet of paper.[10] In addition, it's important to explore your 'blind spots' (known to others but not you). Three questions to encourage people to share this information are: what am I like at my best, and what is my impact? what am I like at my worst, and what is my impact? what would I most like me to change, and what would the impact be? This information can then be added to your incident room.
My values and interests	How do these drive and motivate you? These can help to explain our response to different scenarios in our story so far. It is difficult to be in 'thriving' if our interests and values aren't aligned with what we are doing. You can start by listing out what you think are your values, things such as honesty, service or respect. However, our underlying values are often more visible in times of difficulty and can be seen by the choices we have made. You can also list your interests and motivations. When do you feel most energised? What things do you love doing?

My adaptability	This captures your approach to learning, change and taking control. Are there situations do you have a 'fixed' mindset (trying to hide your weaknesses, seeing challenges and other people's success as threatening or trying to 'prove' that you are successful)? Are there situations where you have a 'growth' mindset (seeing challenges as an opportunity to stretch yourself and learn new things, being persistent in mastering new things or looking to constantly 'improve' what you do)? How do you feel about change? In what ways are you proactive about seeking change in order to have a more satisfying working life? How well are you able to adapt your behaviour to meet the demands of different situations?
My view of careers	What is your personal theory of career?[11] How do you think careers 'work'? What do we think helps people to get on and what holds people back? How do you make decisions, and how do you involve other people? If you believe that people get on by 'keeping their head down and working hard', you are less likely to be proactive about talking to people about what we do and what we want, making it less likely that we will be offered the opportunities that we would really value. Similarly, if our view is that there are few opportunities for 'someone like me', we may undervalue what we have to offer and the contribution we can make.
My current organisation	This context relates to the internal labour market of your organisation and how it matches your attributes.[12] How much of alignment is there between what you want and what your organisation needs? What is the 'fit' between your values and motivators and your current role?[13] What do you enjoy about the culture, and what do you find difficult or frustrating? What types of future opportunities may emerge? How could you find out about and access these opportunities if you were interested in them?
My careerscape[14]	What could impact the nature of opportunities available to you in your current line of work? For example, reflecting on the changes explored in Chapter 2, how could the macrostructures change? How might the internal structures change? What is the likely impact of technological changes? How might the supply of people with your skills, knowledge and experience change? Answering these questions will provide you with additional insights on your employability within and beyond your current organisation. You may consider these as possible scenarios, or you may think in terms of the influence of PESTLIED (political, economic, social, technological, legal, international, environmental and demographic) factors.

F   Life wheel activity to explore goals

Career goals need to be considered within the context of other life goals. The life wheel activity can be used to reflect on your goals for each section. You may want to change some of the headings or add new sections if other things are particularly important to you. Once you have the headings, it is helpful to set a time frame (e.g. five years). Then think what your goals are. What would you like to be happening in each section? Then consider how the different sections interact and any priorities or overriding themes. Next spend a few minutes reflecting: if your goal represents a score of five out of five, what is your current score? This will help you to identify the biggest gaps, and you can identify any actions you want to take. This is a helpful activity to revisit every six months or so to capture any changes.

What are your goals?	Current score	Action
Work		
Health		
Leisure		
Home and family		
Friends		
Finance		
Community		
Personal growth		
Other		

G Options for continued professional development (CPD)

We have shown the importance of CPD for employability. Whilst people intellectually recognise the value and importance of CPD, many people only engage in a limited range of activities to support their development. The following questions are intended to stimulate your thinking about the range of CPD activities you currently engage with and to illustrate the additional opportunities.

The following questions will help you to reflect on which activities you have engaged in, in relation to your CPD <u>in the last 12 months</u>. Indicate your choice by a (tick) or (x), using the following scale:

Never used for my CPD	Rarely used for my CPD	Occasionally used for my CPD	Quite often used for my CPD	Frequently used for my CPD
NEV	RAR	OCC	QUI	FREQ

		NEV	RAR	OCC	QUI	FREQ
1	Learning through practising the rules and procedures of my work organisation	[ ]	[ ]	[ ]	[ ]	[ ]
2	Learning professional knowledge (e.g. professional codes of practice)	[ ]	[ ]	[ ]	[ ]	[ ]
3	Acquiring generic transferable skills and competencies related to my job	[ ]	[ ]	[ ]	[ ]	[ ]
4	Undertaking academic study that isn't necessarily related to my job or profession	[ ]	[ ]	[ ]	[ ]	[ ]
5	Acquiring knowledge through browsing Websites or 'surfing the net'	[ ]	[ ]	[ ]	[ ]	[ ]
6	Exchanging emails on professional topics with colleagues	[ ]	[ ]	[ ]	[ ]	[ ]
7	Taking part in an online discussion forum relevant to my profession	[ ]	[ ]	[ ]	[ ]	[ ]
8	Keeping a reflective diary over an extended period of time	[ ]	[ ]	[ ]	[ ]	[ ]
9	Reflective discussions with colleagues as part of a formal development review process	[ ]	[ ]	[ ]	[ ]	[ ]

10	Reflective discussions with colleagues that are informal but still relevant to my work	[ ]	[ ]	[ ]	[ ]	[ ]
11	My employer's internal training courses	[ ]	[ ]	[ ]	[ ]	[ ]
12	External courses my employer has paid for	[ ]	[ ]	[ ]	[ ]	[ ]
13	My employer's open learning provision	[ ]	[ ]	[ ]	[ ]	[ ]
14	Technical training (e.g. courses where I am learning how to use new computer software)	[ ]	[ ]	[ ]	[ ]	[ ]
15	Working towards a vocational qualification where I am sponsored by my employer	[ ]	[ ]	[ ]	[ ]	[ ]
16	Working towards a vocational qualification which I am paying for myself	[ ]	[ ]	[ ]	[ ]	[ ]
17	Participating in internal secondments or transfers at my place of work	[ ]	[ ]	[ ]	[ ]	[ ]
18	Learning through informal teamwork in the workplace	[ ]	[ ]	[ ]	[ ]	[ ]
19	Sharing knowledge with colleagues	[ ]	[ ]	[ ]	[ ]	[ ]
20	Action learning: learning from development projects	[ ]	[ ]	[ ]	[ ]	[ ]
21	Membership of committees at my place of work (e.g. quality, health and safety)	[ ]	[ ]	[ ]	[ ]	[ ]
22	Reading work-related documents from my organisation	[ ]	[ ]	[ ]	[ ]	[ ]
23	Keeping a portfolio record of CPD activities I have undertaken	[ ]	[ ]	[ ]	[ ]	[ ]
24	Regular reading of websites and books relevant to my profession	[ ]	[ ]	[ ]	[ ]	[ ]
25	Authorship of technical papers (internal or external to the organisation)	[ ]	[ ]	[ ]	[ ]	[ ]
26	Attending professional branch meetings regularly	[ ]	[ ]	[ ]	[ ]	[ ]
27	Coaching, where I am being coached	[ ]	[ ]	[ ]	[ ]	[ ]
28	Coaching, where I am the coach	[ ]	[ ]	[ ]	[ ]	[ ]
29	Other personal activities outside of work (e.g. hobbies, scouts/guides, community or religious organisations, volunteering, etc.)	[ ]	[ ]	[ ]	[ ]	[ ]
30	Learning that is carefully planned in advance	[ ]	[ ]	[ ]	[ ]	[ ]
31	Spontaneous learning arising from work or personal activities	[ ]	[ ]	[ ]	[ ]	[ ]
32	Learning from apps or other digital media	[ ]	[ ]	[ ]	[ ]	[ ]
33	What is the main professional or work-related area, competence or skill that you wish to develop during the next few years?					

Notes

1 For a brief summary on internal communications, visit www.forbes.com/sites/forbesagencycouncil/2016/08/12/best-practices-for-effective-internal-communications/#71d9e7ec7292 (accessed 12.02.2019).

2 For more information on research into the impact of these career skills, see Akkermans, J., Brenninkmeijer, V., Schaufeli, W.B. and Blonk, R.W., 2015. It's all about CareerSKILLS: Effectiveness of a career development intervention for young employees. *Human Resource Management, 54*(4), pp. 533–551.

3 For further information on this research (conducted by Dave Ulrich and Jessica Johnson), see http://rblip.s3.amazonaws.com/Articles/Winning%20Tomorrow%27s%20Talent%20Battle.pdf (accessed 24.06.2019).

4 For example, using the principles of 'contagious communication', Berger, J., 2016. *Contagious: Why things catch on.* London: Simon and Schuster.

5 Developed in the 1980s and 1990s, this was popularised by Sire John Whitmore (among others). Whitmore's influential book, *Coaching for Performance: The Principles and Practice of Coaching and Leadership,* has a special twenty-fifth anniversary edition, published by Nicholas Brealey Publishing in 2017.

6 The idea of 'Nudge' has been popularised, for example, through the influential book on the topic: Leonard, T.C., 2008. Thaler, R.H. and Sunstein, C.R., *Nudge: Improving decisions about health, wealth, and happiness.* London: Penguin Books.

7 This approach has been very successfully applied through work on 'Actionable Conversations' to support habit change. For more information, visit https://performance-1.co.uk/coaching/actionable-conversations/ (accessed 30.04.2019).

8 As suggested by Peter Honey, 'Establishing a learning regime', in *The Best of Peter Honey: A collection of forty articles on behaviour, learning and training* 1997, published by Dr Peter Honey.

9 This was developed by Joe Luft and Harry Ingram in 1961. It is widely quoted as a tool to build self-awareness and deepen relationships. Luft, J. and Ingham, H., 1961. The Johari Window. *Human Relations Training News, 5*(1), 6–7.

10 For example, the 'signature strengths' identified in Seligman, M.E., 2004. *Authentic happiness: Using the new positive psychology to realize your potential for lasting fulfilment.* London: Simon and Schuster. For a list of ninety-two possible strengths, see https://positivepsychologyprogram.com/what-are-your-strengths/ (accessed 30.04.2019). Marc Effron's book, 2018. *8 Steps to high performance.* Boston: Harvard Business Review Press, also has some excellent checklists and activities to support greater awareness of current strengths.

11 This has been termed our 'career world view', see Bosley, S. L., Arnold, J. and Cohen, L., 2009. How other people shape our careers: A typology drawn from career narratives. *Human Relations, 62*(10), 1487–1520.

12 For a model of employability, looking at the internal and external labour markets and how this relates to personal and occupational attributes, see Rothwell, A. and Arnold, J., 2007. Self-perceived employability: Development and validation of a scale. *Personnel Review, 36*(1), 23–41.

13 There has been considerable research on person-organisation fit. This seems to suggest that a high perceived 'fit' is associated with higher performance, organisational commitment and positive organisational citizenship behaviours. For example, see Boon, C., Den Hartog, D. N., Boselie, P. and Paauwe, J., 2011. The relationship between perceptions of HR practices and employee outcomes: Examining the role of person – organisation and person – job fit. *The International Journal of Human Resource Management, 22*(1), 138–162.

14 The term 'careerscape' is used in Inkson, K., Dries, N. and Arnold, J., 2014. *Understanding careers: Metaphors of working lives.* London: Sage, 294.

Index

Note: Page numbers in *italic* indicate a figure and page numbers in **bold** indicate a table on the corresponding page.

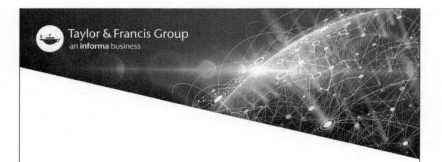